ALL THE BEST PIZZAS

ALL THE BEST

PIZZAS

B Y

JOIE WARNER

HEARST BOOKS • New York

A FLAVOR BOOK

LIBRARY OF CONGRESS CATALOGING-IN-PUBLICATION DATA
Warner, Joie
    All the best pizzas/by Joie Warner.
        p.   cm.
Includes index.
ISBN 0-688-10125-9
1.Pizza   1. Title
TX770.P58W37   1991
641.8'24-dc20   90-42484
                                                    CIP

Printed in the United States of America
    4 5 6 7 8 9 10

This book was created and produced by

Flavor Publications, Inc.
208 East 51st Street, Suite 240
New York, New York 10022

DEDICATED TO my favorite *pizzaiolos:*
Frank, Salvatore, Joe, Pete, Ed, Wolf, and Alice and to my
pizza tasters: Drew, Ella, Ken, Kristina, Peter, Gregg, Sue,
Marty, Kimberly, Charles, Paula, Terri, and Jerry.

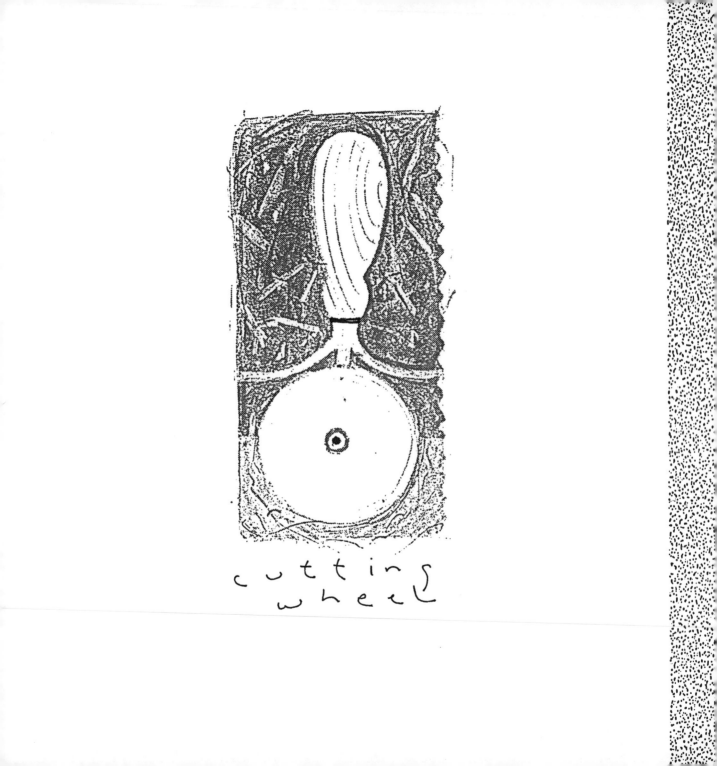

cutting
wheel

CONTENTS

I N T R O D U C T I O N

PIZZA is taking America by storm...again. Only this time it's not Italian per se, but American. Just a few years ago pizza meant the ubiquitous Neapolitan-style specialty of baked dough topped with tomato sauce, mozzarella, and pepperoni, but today's pizzas, sometimes referred to as "gourmet pizzas" or "designer pizzas," are very sophisticated, artistically assembled, and topped with exotic ingredients such as wild mushrooms, goat cheese, sun-dried tomatoes, pesto, fiery red peppers, or grilled vegetables. Many do not have any tomato sauce or cheese – a definite change from the pizza parlor mentality. The crusts are thin and chewy or cracker-crisp and are usually no larger than a dinner plate. Drizzled with the best olive oils and dusted with fresh herbs and quality cheese, these ultra-appetizing pizzettas have gained new cachet.

Restaurants such as Chez Panisse and Spago in California began the trend by baking single-serving mini-pizzas in brick ovens fired by maple or oak. California-style, upscale pizzerias are now flourishing all across America. This is not to say that the old standby, "mushroom, green pepper, pepperoni, extra cheese" pizza is no longer. As a matter of fact, the all-time favorite pizza topping in America is pepperoni, followed by mushrooms and sausage.

Historians say that pizza, like pasta, is one of the oldest of foods. But Neapolitans claim that it was created in Naples with the arrival of the tomato in the 1800s. And it's true that the pizza that gained worldwide popularity had its roots in Naples. The earliest pizzas were rustic flattened breads, topped with simple ingredients like olive oil and garlic or herbs, made fresh to order, and cooked in clay-lined brick ovens that reached very high temperatures (we've obviously come full circle!). They are still cooked the same way in Italy today with regional variations in crusts and toppings.

When pizza landed on American shores, it was adopted and glorified to such an extent that many believe it was actually an American creation. At any rate, it is obvious that Americans are truly enthusiastic about pizza.

Contrary to popular belief, pizza-making is not at all difficult. Pizzas can very easily be made at home. The dough can be turned out in seconds using a food processor (or by hand if preferred), the sauce whipped up in minutes, the toppings added, then baked in a very hot oven for 5 to 10 minutes.

But why make pizza at home, you ask, when there is a pizza parlor on almost every corner? Simply because homemade pizza tastes so much better than restaurant pizza. The home cook can select the freshest produce, real cheeses, and best-quality olive oils, which makes homemade pizza not only delicious, but more nutritious, too. Not only that, once the dough has risen, a pizza can be assembled and baked in less time than it takes for an ordered pizza to arrive at your door.

All the Best Pizzas is a collection of my favorite pizza recipes. I've been a passionate pizza-maker for a long time, and this book is the result of years of experimenting with numerous doughs and toppings. Most of my recipes have been inspired by the pizzas I have tasted all over America. I've enjoyed pizza topped with smoked salmon and caviar at Spago in Los Angeles; deep-dish pizza at Gino's and spinach soufflé pizza at Edwardo's in Chicago; sausage pizza at Santarpio's in Boston; and mushroom, green pepper, and onion pizza at John's in New York City.

I fell in love with Pepe's white clam pizza cooked in a huge coal oven in New Haven, Connecticut, and have devoured myriad pizzas topped with good old-fashioned pepperoni et al, in pizzerias all over New York state.

In the following chapters you will find everything you need to know about making perfect crusts, simple sauces, and classic to exotic toppings, such as Braised Garlic, Pancetta, and Fresh Basil; Tuna, Roasted Red Peppers, and Capers; Chili with Sour Cream and Green Onions; Smoked Salmon and Caviar; Goat Cheese and Sun-Dried Tomatoes; Italian Sausage and Hot Peppers; Cheddar Cheese and Bacon; Braised Onions and Gorgonzola; and, of course, that favorite of favorites, Pepperoni. Supplementing the recipes is a glossary of ingredients plus practical hints on proper baking techniques and necessary equipment. Once the basics are mastered, you'll find out how easy it is to create your own pizzas.

Pizzas are tasty, versatile, wholesome, inexpensive, informal, fun to make, and equally fun to eat. I know that once you make your own, you'll never eat pizza-parlor pizza again.

JOIE WARNER

BASICS

THE DOUGH

The dough contributes as much to the quality of the pizza as the toppings. A perfect crust is light, crisp, and slightly chewy. This is achieved by using the right flour, kneading, rising, and shaping the dough properly, and baking in a hot, preferably brick-lined oven.

The best flour for a well-textured crust is bread flour or unbleached all-purpose flour. You can make perfectly acceptable crusts with bleached all-purpose flour, but the higher gluten content of bread and unbleached flours results in superlative crusts. Because they absorb more water, the dough expands more. Even though whole-wheat flour is healthier, it is not traditional, and I find it overpowers the delicate flavors of the toppings. If you want to make a whole-wheat dough, remove a half cup bread flour and replace it with whole-wheat flour.

Active dry yeast — not the fresh variety — is used in the recipes in this book because it is more readily available and I have found no discernible difference between them. It is important when dissolving yeast not to use too hot or too cold water — the yeast will either be killed by the heat or inactivated by the cold. Err on the side of cool (75 to 80 degrees) rather than too warm, because a slower rise produces the best crust.

A little sugar is "fed" to the yeast first; then it should stand for 10 minutes until foamy. If it doesn't foam, the yeast is no longer effective or the temperature of the water was incorrect.

The next step is to knead the dough to develop the gluten in the flour. I make my dough in a food processor. I add the flour and salt, then with the motor running, add the yeast mixture through the feed tube. (It's easy to mix the dough in a bowl by hand – just a bit messier.) The dough should be a little sticky. Do not add more flour unless absolutely necessary, because the less flour used, the more tender the crust Remove the dough from the processor and place on a lightly floured surface. Knead until smooth and shiny and no longer sticky. Use a dough scraper if necessary to scrape any that sticks to the board instead of adding more flour. To knead the dough, give it some "rough treatment." Knead for 10 seconds, then take the ball of dough and throw it down hard onto the surface 5 to 10 times. Continue kneading and throwing 3 or 4 more times until it is no longer sticky. Lightly coat the dough with olive or vegetable oil and place in bowl large enough to allow the dough to double in volume (preferably a bowl with high sides rather than wide to assist the dough in rising). Cover the bowl with plastic wrap, sealing it completely, or the dough will form a hard crust.

Set the bowl at room temperature (not in a warm oven) and let rise for a minimum of 1 hour. I usually make my dough in the morning and let it rise, then refrigerate several hours until dinner time. Do not punch the dough down! The long single rise gives it a rustic and chewy texture and wonderful yeasty flavor.

Once it has risen, you may use the dough immediately or refrigerate it for up to 4 days. Gently push down the dough, remove it from the bowl, and slice it into 2 to 4 equal pieces (or leave whole for a 14-inch pizza). Wrap each piece in plastic wrap – not too tightly (leaving enough space for the dough to expand) but completely. If not using immediately, refrigerate. I find the texture on the second day improved over the first day and the dough easier to handle. You will notice a textural change each day and may find you prefer dough made on the first, second, third, or fourth day. Each day it loses some moisture so that when baked, the crusts become drier and crisper. I never freeze my dough, but you may double-wrap and freeze it for 1 to 2 weeks – no longer

SHAPING

Hand stretching the dough produces the most tender, chewy crust. Unless you are very careful, the rolling pin method flattens out the air bubbles, making the edges of the crust hard and tough. A hand-stretched dough puffs up beautifully around the edges, giving the pizza a rustic look and texture. It takes practice, but do try it a few times before giving up!

There are two ways to hand shape. My favorite technique is to flour my hands and the counter lightly, then place the dough on the counter and flatten it slightly. I place the dough on an open palm, then pass it back and forth from one open palm to the other, slapping my hands together as I am stretching the dough. The dough will get thinner and larger as it is passed between your palms. Another way is to pick up the slightly flattened dough with both hands, holding the edges of the circle. Turn, pull, and stretch it all at the same time, turning it like a steering wheel. Gravity helps pull the dough as you are turning.

Once the dough is hand stretched to about a 7-inch circle or 11-inch for a 14-inch pizza (if it won't stretch and keeps retracting, let it rest for 5 minutes and try again), place it back on a lightly floured surface. Press it out further with your fingertips, turning it at the same time, another 1 to 2 inches, being careful not to make the dough too thin in the center. It should be about 1/8 inch thick except for the edges, which will puff up during baking.

Place the dough on a floured baker's peel or an oiled pizza pan and push it out further with your hands until it is 10 inches (or 14 inches) in diameter, keeping edges thicker.

If shaping by hand is too difficult, then by all means use a rolling pin to flatten the dough into a circle.

Don't worry if the dough circle isn't perfectly round – a slightly uneven shape gives it a rustic look. To transfer the dough circle to a peel or pan, place a rolling pin at the top of the dough; gently roll the dough over the rolling pin, then place on pan or peel and unroll.

Next, brush the surface of the dough (I use my hands) with a little olive oil before adding the toppings. This will prevent sogginess. The toppings should not be runny or the sauces too thin or they will soak into the crust, making it soggy.

Toppings

Topping possibilities are endless, from the most traditional (tomato sauce, cheese, and pepperoni) to the most exotic (hoisin sauce and Chinese barbecued pork or duck). I tend towards traditional, but by all means try your own combinations. I'm not usually keen on fruit as a topping, though you might love pineapple and chicken. Really, anything goes as long as you use the freshest ingredients and keep the toppings very simple. Try to stay with 3 or 4 toppings at most, although there are exceptions. Many of my pizza toppings have only 2 or 3 ingredients, because I think simple is better

Baking

The best crusts are baked in brick ovens, preferably heated by wood or coal. Most homes don't have wood-burning ovens, but that shouldn't deter you from making delicious pizza. For an authentic texture I recommend that you use unglazed quarry tiles or a pizza stone, placed on an open rack to approximate a commercial brick oven. Measure your oven and purchase enough tiles to line the rack. The tiles must first be heated in a very hot oven — 500 degrees, or as hot as your oven will go — for an hour before the pizza is baked. The tiles and stone retain enough heat to absorb moisture from the crust, making it light and chewy. The pizza is baked directly on the tiles.

A long-handled baker's peel is needed to slide the pizza in and out of the oven. This takes a little practice to correctly jerk the pizza from peel to tiles. Be sure to lightly dust the peel with flour or cornmeal before placing the dough on it. Place the dough at the front edge and give it a gentle jerk to test whether the pizza will slide off easily. Work very quickly, adding toppings and getting the pizza into the oven before it sticks to the peel. Do not use the peel with any pizzas that have heavy toppings, or the pizza will be too heavy to slide off the peel.

If you are not using a pizza stone or tiles, I recommend black steel pizza pans (not deep-dish pans, unless you are baking a deep-dish pizza) because they hold the heat better than shiny aluminum pans. The crusts will be almost as crispy-chewy as those cooked in a tile-lined oven, but shiny aluminum pans will give you crusts that are doughy and uncooked on the bottom.

If you can't find unglazed quarry tiles (available at ceramic tile dealers), pizza stones, or black pizza pans (available at restaurant supply stores or kitchen shops), then beg them to order one for you. They make all the difference in the world.

QUANTITIES

Ten-inch pizzas are single-serving size. When I serve two to four people I always bake two to four pizzas, each with different toppings. Everyone can share a slice while the next ones are being prepared and baked – or bake one 14-inch pizza, having doubled the topping ingredients accordingly.

INGREDIENTS

ANCHOVIES: My recipes use the canned anchovy fillets in oil. Some brands are saltier than others, so experiment until you find a brand you like.

ARTICHOKE HEARTS: Both canned and marinated artichokes are available in most supermarkets and specialty stores. They are interchangeable on pizza, but they do differ in flavor. Marinated artichokes are prepared with oil and herbs, while canned artichokes are packed only in brine. You must drizzle the tops of canned artichokes with olive oil before baking, or they will dry out.

BLACK OLIVES: For pizza, I prefer Kalamata olives from Greece or Niçoise olives from France. They are available in specialty food shops and many super-market delis. Canned American olives do not have the flavor or pungency needed for the recipes in this book.

BLACK PEPPER: I always use freshly ground black peppercorns, because pre-ground pepper has little flavor.

CAPERS: These are the unopened flower buds of a Mediterranean shrub. Many cooks prefer the tiny French capers, but I use the large variety on my pizzas because they have a stronger flavor. They are packed in vinegar (not salt), and I never rinse them.

CAVIAR: Because salmon roe is very perishable, it should be bought frozen and thawed just before using. Salmon roe comes from Pacific salmon. It is also called red caviar, and is available from quality fish stores and most well-stocked food shops.

CORIANDER: A pungent herb also known as cilantro or Chinese parsley.

GARLIC: I'm sure no one would ever consider sprinkling powdered garlic over pizza, but just in case...DON'T! That goes for pizza sauce, too. Always use fresh garlic; choose large bulbs that are firm to the touch and not sprouting.

GORGONZOLA: A very creamy, mold-ripened cheese from the Lombardy region of Italy. It is best to use a young, mild Gorgonzola for pizza. It is available in Italian food shops or well-stocked cheese stores.

MOZZARELLA: Sometimes referred to as "pizza cheese," because of its popularity and perfect melting qualities. The finest Italian mozzarella, mozzarella di bufala, is made from buffalo's milk. It is difficult to obtain in North America. American versions are made from cow's milk, and the best type for pizza is *low-moisture* mozzarella, which contains about 40 to 52 percent moisture. It is available in Italian food shops and most supermarkets. The brand I purchase is shrink-wrapped in the shape of a ball about the size of an orange. Whole-milk mozzarella is best for pizza-making, because of its melting qualities. *Fresh mozzarella* is made by hand and has a lovely fresh, mild flavor. Substitute fresh mozzarella for low-moisture whenever possible. For topping pizza, it must be sliced rather than grated. It is found soaking in water in Italian food shops and is quite perishable, so use it within a day or two. The familiar *part-skim* mozzarella found in supermarkets is bland and rubbery. It is acceptable if the other types are not available.

OLIVE OIL: Use a good-quality (not necessarily expensive), fruit-flavored oil for drizzling on top of pizza and oiling pans. Try different brands until you find one you like.

PANCETTA: An Italian-style bacon that is unsmoked, seasoned with pepper and spices, then rolled. It is found mainly in Italian food shops.

PINE NUTS (pignoli): These small, mild, sweet nuts do not have any substitutes. They go rancid quite quickly, so I usually refrigerate or freeze them. They are available in most specialty food shops and some supermarkets.

PROSCIUTTO: This salted, dried Italian ham is available in Italian food shops and some supermarket delis. Don't purchase if it appears hard and dried out around the edges

PROVOLONE: My favorite pizza cheese. Mixed with mozzarella, it gives a pizza an incredible flavor, and it melts beautifully, too. Be sure to purchase Italian provolone rather than domestic, because it has a fuller, more complex flavor. It is available at well-stocked cheese stores, in many supermarkets (especially if they are near Italian neighborhoods), and Italian food shops.

RED ONION: Use the delicate-flavored red onion (sliced paper thin) on pizzas, rather than the stronger cooking onion.

RICOTTA: Fresh ricotta is a soft, white curd cheese that resembles cottage cheese, but it is finer in taste and texture. Depending on the brand used, some need to be drained for an hour or so, because if there is too much liquid, it will soak into the pizza crust, making it soggy.

SHALLOTS: These have a delicate onion-garlic flavor. If unavailable, I often substitute a little minced garlic and onion.

SQUID: To clean, gently pull the head and body apart. Cut off the tentacles just in front of the eyes. Squeeze out the beak, located where tentacles come together (it looks like a small white marble) and discard. Under cold running water, remove all the entrails inside the body sac. Peel off the purple membrane covering the body. Rinse the tentacles and follow the recipe instructions.

TOMATOES, CANNED: The best canned tomatoes come from the San Marzano region in Italy, but they are difficult to find. Buy the best Italian or domestic brands available (experiment until you find a brand you like), since this will make an enormous difference in the taste and quality of your sauces.

TOMATOES, FRESH: Use only flavorful, ripe, unwaxed tomatoes. If they are not fully ripe when you purchase them, do not refrigerate; instead, allow the tomatoes to ripen at room temperature. Sliced, fresh tomatoes must be seeded and drained well before being added to pizza, or the liquid will seep out and make the dough soggy.

TOMATOES, SUN-DRIED: These have become very popular in North America in the past few years. Their intense tomato taste is a wonderful addition to sauces, salads, and pizzas. Pumate San Remo from Liguria, Italy, is considered the best brand. They are available in most specialty food shops.

WILD MUSHROOMS: Many fresh exotic fungi are now available at specialty food shops. *Oyster mushrooms* are cultivated and also grown wild. The flesh is firm and white or gray in color. *Shiitake mushrooms* are an umbrella-shaped, brownish-black variety that were once only available dried. *Cèpes/porcini* have a sweet, nutty flavor and are available mostly in the fall. *Chanterelles*, egg-yolk colored and funnel-shaped, have a delicate but distinct flavor with a slight apricot aroma. *Morels* are considered by many to be the peerless mushroom. They are pitted like a honeycomb and have a tendency to trap sand. Wash them carefully, but quickly and do not allow them to soak.

EQUIPMENT

CHEESE GRATER: For grating cheeses, from hard cheeses like Parmesan, to soft cheeses like mozzarella. I prefer to hand grate rather than grate in a food processor, because the food processor tends to mash the cheese, which changes its melting qualities.

CUTTING WHEEL: These have sturdy handles, blade guards, and blades that are around 3 inches in diameter. I prefer a professional cutter (Dexter brand), which is all metal with replaceable blades. They are available at restaurant supply stores.

DOUGH SCRAPER: The scraper with its hardwood or plastic handle and stainless-steel square blade is especially made for scraping up the sticky dough from the counter or work surface. It is available at kitchenware shops.

FOOD PROCESSOR: Although I don't use my processor to grate cheese, it is indispensable for making doughs and sauces.

LARGE MIXING BOWL: The best bowls for holding rising pizza dough have high sides (about 6½ inches high). If you have a Kitchen Aid mixer, the stainless-steel mixing bowl works perfectly for dough rising. Bowls must be large enough for the dough to triple in volume.

OLIVE OIL CAN: Not absolutely necessary, but it makes the task of drizzling oil onto your pizza much easier than pouring straight out of the bottle. Available in restaurant supply stores or Italian specialty shops.

PEPPER MILL: Essential for cooking and at the table.

PIZZA PANS: The best pizzas are cooked directly on baking stones or tiles. The second-best method is to cook pizzas on pans made of black steel, rather than shiny aluminum pans. Black steel pans retain more heat, producing crisper crusts. Never use shiny aluminum pans.

PIZZA PEEL: A long-handled tool made out of wood or part metal with a flat paddle-shaped foot, for transferring pizza to and from a brick-lined oven. Don't purchase one that is too long or large; measure the space between your oven and counter so that you can move the peel freely. Once you get the knack of maneuvering the pizza with the proper jerky movements, you'll feel like a real professional, and your guests will be very impressed. (Besides, it is the only way to make truly outstanding pizzas.)

PIZZA SPATULA: Pizza serving spatulas are for transferring slices of pizza to plates. They are available at cookware shops and restaurant supply stores.

ROLLING PIN: If you find hand stretching the dough difficult, you will need a rolling pin for rolling out pizza dough.

SERRATED KNIVES: If you're not from the old school of eating pizza with your hands (the way pizza was meant to be eaten!), set the table with forks and serrated knives (such as steak knives with serrated edges), because they cut through the crust more easily.

UNGLAZED TILES OR BAKING STONE: To convert your oven into a pizza oven, buy unglazed quarry tiles from a ceramic tile dealer or baking stones from a cookware shop. The clay retains intense heat, which absorbs the moisture from the crust, giving the pizza an evenly browned and crisp bottom crust. The tiles or stone must be preheated for an hour in a 500°F to 550°F oven. Purchase tiles that are just under 1/2 inch thick. Thick ones take too long to heat, and thinner ones can crack from the intense heat. To clean the tiles and stones, do not use detergent, because it clogs the pores. Just rinse and scrub well with hot water. The tiles will blacken with time and may eventually have to be replaced.

NOTE: Each of the following toppings is for a 10-inch pizza. If you wish to make a 14-inch pizza, use all of the dough, but double the topping ingredients or increase to taste.

PIZZA DOUGHS

◆ ◆ ◆

Years ago, I began experimenting with different doughs in search of the perfect pizza crust. This dough and Thin and Crispy Dough are pretty close to perfection, I think.
♦ Rustic Dough can be used for either thin- or thick-crust pizzas. It's also more breadlike and chewier than Thin and Crispy Dough. Both doughs can be used interchangeably, although it is best to use Rustic Dough with heavier toppings and Thin and Crispy Dough with lighter ones. ♦ Please read the Basics chapter before making and shaping the crusts. ♦ It is important to oil the pizza pan lightly and then wipe out the excess oil — there should be only a very thin film — before placing the dough on the pan; otherwise the crust will be greasy.

RUSTIC DOUGH

1 envelope dry yeast
   (2½ teaspoons)
¼ teaspoon sugar
¾ cup lukewarm water

1¾ cups bread flour
   or unbleached
   all-purpose flour
½ teaspoon salt
Olive oil

IN A 1-CUP MEASURING CUP or bowl, stir yeast and sugar into water. Set aside for 10 minutes, or until foamy. Stir again.

Meanwhile, add flour and salt to a food processor. With motor running, pour yeast mixture through feed tube and continue processing until dough forms into a ball, about 10 to 20 seconds. (If dough needs a little more water to combine, add it a tablespoon at a time.) The dough should be a little sticky. Do not add more flour. (To make dough by hand, add yeast mixture to flour and salt in a large bowl and knead until dough is combined.)

Turn dough out onto a lightly floured surface. Pick up dough

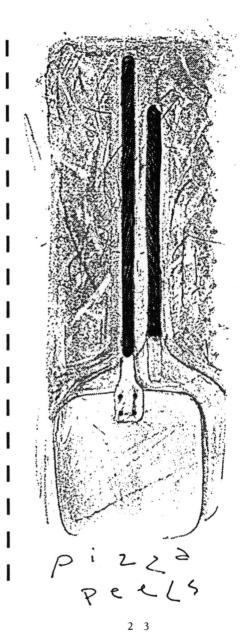

pizza peels

and throw it down hard 8 or 9 times, using dough scraper to scrape up any stuck to the surface. Knead several times, dusting with a little flour at this point if dough is still too sticky to handle, and throw down again 8 or 9 times, continuing throwing and kneading until smooth and no longer sticky, about 1 to 2 minutes.

Lightly oil dough and place in a bowl (preferably with high sides) large enough to allow it to double in volume. Cover bowl tightly with plastic wrap. Let stand at room temperature for at least 1 hour, or until doubled in volume. You may also refrigerate for several hours or overnight. Do not punch dough down.

With floured hands, gently pull dough down from sides of bowl, remove, and slice into 2 equal sections (or leave whole for a 14-inch pizza). Use immediately or wrap each section well in plastic wrap (leaving enough room for expansion); place in refrigerator for up to 4 days.

Makes about 1 pound dough, enough for two 10-inch pizzas or one 14-inch pizza

E very connoisseur knows that the secret to great pizza is the crust. Here is a close facsimile of the thin and crispy crusts that are served in all the "gourmet" pizzerias. ◆ Divide dough into five equal pieces instead of four, and roll each piece into a 10-inch circle for the thinnest, crispiest crust ever.

THIN AND CRISPY DOUGH

1 envelope dry yeast
  (2½ teaspoons)
¼ teaspoon sugar
¾ cup lukewarm water
2½ cups bread flour
  or unbleached
  all-purpose flour

½ teaspoon salt
1 large egg
Olive oil

IN A 1-CUP MEASURING CUP or bowl, stir yeast and sugar into water. Set aside for 10 minutes, or until foamy. Stir again
    Meanwhile, add flour and salt to a food processor.
    Lightly beat egg into yeast mixture With motor running, pour yeast mixture through feed tube, and continue processing until dough forms into a ball, about 10 to 20 seconds. (If dough needs a little more water, add it a tablespoon at a time.) The dough should be a little sticky. Do not add more flour. (To make dough by hand, add yeast

mixture to flour and salt in a large bowl and knead until dough is combined.)

Turn dough out onto a lightly floured surface. Pick up dough and throw it down hard 8 or 9 times, using dough scraper to scrape up any stuck to the surface. Knead several times, dusting with a little flour at this point if dough is still too sticky to handle after kneading, and throw down again 8 or 9 times, continuing throwing and kneading until smooth and no longer sticky, about 1 to 2 minutes

Lightly oil dough and place in a bowl (preferably with high sides) large enough to allow it to double in volume. Cover bowl tightly with plastic wrap. Let stand at room temperature for at least 1 hour, or until doubled in volume. You may also refrigerate dough several hours or overnight. Do not punch dough down.

With floured hands, gently pull dough down from sides of bowl, remove, and slice into 4 equal sections (or leave whole for a 14-inch pizza). Use immediately or wrap each section well in plastic wrap (leaving enough room for expansion); place in refrigerator for up to 4 days.

Makes about 1¹/₂ pounds dough, enough for four 10-inch pizzas or one 14-inch pizza

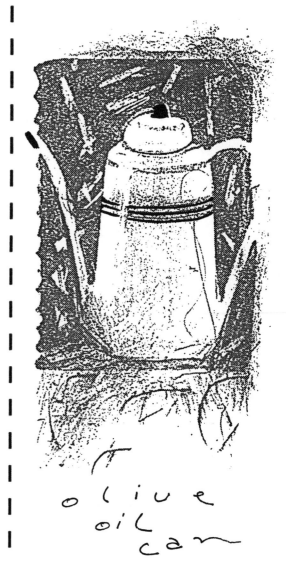

olive oil can

PIZZA SAUCES

♦ ♦ ♦

NO-COOK TOMATO SAUCE

1 large garlic clove	4 large fresh basil
1 can (28 ounces) tomatoes	leaves, chopped
About 4 tablespoons tomato	1/4 teaspoon hot red
paste	pepper flakes
1/2 teaspoon sugar	1/4 teaspoon freshly ground
1/2 teaspoon salt	black pepper
1 teaspoon dried oregano	

IN A FOOD PROCESSOR, mince garlic.

Place a strainer over a bowl and drain tomatoes by gently pressing and crushing them with a wooden spoon to remove most, but not all, liquid.

Transfer crushed tomatoes to the food processor and discard or save liquid in bowl for another use. Add tomato paste (adjusting it to the amount of liquid remaining in the drained tomatoes – sauce must not be too thick *or* too runny), sugar, and salt and process ingredients a few seconds to combine. Transfer to a nonaluminum bowl. Stir in oregano, basil, hot pepper flakes, and pepper. Cover and refrigerate until using.

Makes about 1 1/2 cups.

A sauce that is so quick and easy, there is no excuse to use bottled sauce on your pizza ever again. ♦ You may combine all the ingredients in the food processor, but I like to stir in the herbs separately to keep the tomatoes brightly colored.

The vegetables should be cooked only until most of the liquid is evaporated and the vegetables are soft, but with their individual textures and flavors still intact. ◆ This sauce is for Ratatouille Pizza (see page 54).

RATATOUILLE

¼ cup olive oil
1 pound eggplant, unpeeled and cubed
3 medium zucchini, unpeeled and sliced
1 large onion, thinly sliced
2 sweet red peppers, seeded and coarsely chopped
6 large garlic cloves, chopped

3 very large ripe tomatoes (about 1½ pounds) seeded and diced
1 teaspoon dried thyme
1 teaspoon dried basil or oregano
Salt
Freshly ground black pepper
¾ cup finely chopped fresh parsley

IN A LARGE heavy skillet, heat oil. Add eggplant and cook for 5 minutes, or until soft. Add zucchini, onion, red peppers, and garlic and cook for 5 minutes, or until onion is soft. Add tomatoes, thyme, basil, salt, and pepper. Simmer for 20 minutes and stir in parsley. Cook for 5 minutes more, or until most of the liquid has evaporated.

Makes about 4 cups.

PESTO SAUCE

1 large garlic clove	⅓ cup freshly grated
2 tablespoons pine nuts	Parmesan cheese
1 cup fresh basil leaves	¼ cup olive oil
(packed)	

IN A FOOD PROCESSOR, mince garlic. Add pine nuts, basil, and cheese. Continue processing, adding oil in a stream through feed tube. Taste for seasoning and adjust if necessary.

Makes about ¾ cup.

L*eftover pesto may be refrigerated in a jar, covered with a film of olive oil.*
♦ *This sauce is for Pesto Pizza (see page 50).*

Gourmet pizzerias often bring a bottle of spicy oil to the table for drizzling over baked pizzas. ◆ Many pizzas are enhanced by the addition of this flavored oil. Pass it at the table for each person to drizzle to taste.

SPICY OIL

1 cup olive oil
½ teaspoon whole black
  peppercorns
1 tablespoon fresh rosemary
  leaves

3 to 4 dried red chilies, or to
  taste
1 large garlic clove, peeled
  and smashed with the flat
  side of a cleaver

IN A HEAVY SMALL SKILLET, heat oil. Add peppercorns, rosemary, dried red chilies, and garlic. Cook for 4 minutes, or until garlic begins to sizzle. Immediately remove from heat. Do not allow garlic to brown, or oil will be bitter. Set aside and cool to room temperature. Pour all ingredients into sterilized bottle with spout.

Makes about 1 cup.

TRADITIONAL

PIZZAS

♦ ♦ ♦

H istory tells us that this is the oldest of pizzas. Very basic, yet exceedingly good, it was traditionally served as an accompaniment to pasta; serve it with a meal in place of garlic bread. ♦ The crust puffs up not only on the edges, but throughout the center of the pizza, giving it an authentic, rustic look. ♦ As a variation, you can add fresh or dried herbs such as oregano, sage, or rosemary.

OIL AND GARLIC PIZZA

Prepared dough, enough for   3 to 4 large garlic cloves,
  one 10-inch pizza   finely chopped
1 tablespoon olive oil   ⅛ teaspoon coarse salt

LINE OVEN RACK with quarry tiles or pizza stone if using. Preheat oven to 500°F for 1 hour.

Sprinkle peel with cornmeal or flour, or lightly coat a black pizza pan with olive oil.

Hand stretch or roll out dough into a 10-inch circle and place on peel or pan.

In a small bowl, toss olive oil and garlic together, then spread over dough, leaving a ½-inch border. Sprinkle with salt.

Bake for 5 minutes, or until crust is golden.

PIZZA MARGHERITA

Prepared dough, enough for one 10-inch pizza	1 ripe medium tomato (about ¼ pound), seeded and diced
Olive oil	Salt
½ cup grated fontina cheese	1 tablespoon freshly grated Parmesan cheese
¼ cup grated provolone cheese	2 tablespoons finely shredded fresh basil leaves
¼ cup grated mozzarella cheese	

LINE OVEN RACK with quarry tiles or pizza stone if using. Preheat oven to 500°F for 1 hour.

Sprinkle peel with cornmeal or flour, or lightly coat a black pizza pan with olive oil.

Hand stretch or roll out dough into a 10-inch circle and place on peel or pan. Brush dough lightly with oil to cover completely.

Spread cheeses over dough, leaving a ½-inch border. Top with tomato and salt lightly.

Bake for 5 to 10 minutes, or until cheese is flecked with golden-brown spots.

Remove pizza from oven. Sprinkle with Parmesan cheese and basil leaves.

The essence of simplicity, this traditional pizza was invented and named for Italy's Queen Margherita in the 1800s. ◆ It is gorgeous and refined and, if one didn't know any better, one would think it had been created by a trendy California chef in the 1980s.

After the Neapolitan pizza, this is one of the most traditional of pizzas. ♦ For anchovy lovers only

MARINARA PIZZA

Prepared dough, enough for
    one 10-inch pizza
Olive oil
½ cup No-Cook Tomato
    Sauce (see page 27)

8 anchovy fillets, drained
1 large garlic clove,
    finely chopped
Freshly ground black pepper

LINE OVEN RACK with quarry tiles or pizza stone if using. Preheat oven to 500°F for 1 hour.

Sprinkle peel with cornmeal or flour, or lightly coat a black pizza pan with olive oil.

Hand stretch or roll out dough into a 10-inch circle and place on peel or pan. Brush dough lightly with oil to cover completely.

Spread tomato sauce over dough, leaving a ½-inch border. Arrange anchovies over sauce in a spoke pattern. Top with garlic and a few grindings of pepper. (Do not salt because the anchovies are salty enough.) Drizzle with 1 teaspoon olive oil.

Bake for 5 to 10 minutes, or until crust is golden

FOCACCIA WITH ROSEMARY, GARLIC, AND COARSE SALT

Prepared Thin and Crispy
  Dough, enough for one
  10-inch pizza
2 medium garlic cloves,
  thinly sliced

2 tablespoons fresh
  rosemary sprigs
1/8 teaspoon coarse salt
2 teaspoons olive oil

LINE OVEN RACK with quarry tiles or pizza stone if using. Preheat oven to 500°F for 1 hour.

Sprinkle peel with cornmeal or flour, or lightly coat a black pizza pan with olive oil.

Hand stretch or roll out dough into a 10-inch circle and place on peel or pan.

Make indentations with your knuckle over surface of dough and place garlic slices and rosemary sprigs in each indentation. Sprinkle with coarse salt and drizzle olive oil over top.

Bake for 5 minutes, or until crust is golden. Be careful not to overcook, or garlic will be bitter. Serve warm or at room temperature.

Focaccia is one of the old, traditional flatbreads from Tuscany. It is eaten for breakfast and snacks and makes a perfect hors d'oeuvre with drinks or a nice change from bread at dinner. ◆ There are many delicious versions, although the following focaccia is garlicky and salty and one of my favorites. ◆ The crust can also be baked "naked," removed from the oven, then simply drizzled with a fruity olive oil, or topped with rings of onions and fresh herbs, or sun-dried tomatoes and fresh herbs and baked.

C

alzone is a filled turnover made with pizza dough and toppings. ♦ Any pizza topping can be used as a filling. ♦ Allow the calzone to cool a little once it is cut open, because it is very hot.

CALZONE WITH PROSCIUTTO, HERBS, AND THREE CHEESES

Prepared dough, enough for one 10-inch pizza
¼ cup No-Cook Tomato Sauce (see page 27)
¼ cup diced mozzarella cheese
½ cup grated fontina cheese
1 tablespoon freshly grated Parmesan cheese
¼ cup coarsely chopped prosciutto
1 large garlic clove, finely chopped
1 tablespoon chopped fresh basil leaves or ½ teaspoon dried
Olive oil

LINE OVEN RACK with quarry tiles or pizza stone if using. Preheat oven to 500°F for 1 hour.

Sprinkle peel with cornmeal or flour, or lightly coat a black pizza pan with olive oil.

Hand stretch or roll out dough into a 10- to 11-inch oval and place on peel or pan.

Spread tomato sauce over half of dough, leaving a 1/2-inch border. Top with cheeses, prosciutto, garlic, and basil.

Moisten the edge of dough with water and fold the other half to form a turnover. Using the tines of a fork, press edges together along edge to seal well. Brush top with olive oil; cut three steam vents in top with a sharp knife.

Bake for 15 minutes, or until turnover is brown and crisp.

Remove calzone from oven and brush again with olive oil. Allow to stand for 5 minutes before serving.

PISSALADIÈRE

Olive oil
2 tablespoons butter
2 large red onions (about
    1½ pounds), thinly sliced
6 large garlic cloves, chopped
2 teaspoons dried thyme
Prepared dough, enough for
    one 10 by 14-inch pizza
    (about ¾ pound dough)

8 anchovy fillets, drained
12 black olives (Niçoise or
    Kalamata), unpitted
1 to 2 tablespoons capers,
    drained
1 tablespoon pine nuts
¼ cup finely chopped fresh
    parsley

PREHEAT OVEN to 500°F for 1 hour.

Lightly coat a large black baking sheet (available at restaurant supply stores) with olive oil.

In a heavy large skillet, heat 3 tablespoons oil with butter. Add onions, garlic, and thyme. Cook on low heat, stirring occasionally, for 25 to 30 minutes, or until soft and caramelized. Set aside.

Hand stretch or roll out dough into a 10 by 14-inch rectangle and place on baking sheet. Brush dough lightly with oil to cover completely. Spread onion mixture over dough, leaving a ½-inch border. Arrange anchovies over onion mixture in a criss-cross pattern. Place olives and capers between anchovies. Sprinkle with pine nuts.

Bake for 10 minutes, or until crust is golden.

Remove pizza from oven and sprinkle with parsley.

A pungent Provençal first cousin to Italian pizza. ◆ Serve as an appetizer or as a light luncheon dish, along with a crisp green salad. ◆ As a variation you may add two large seeded and diced tomatoes to the onion mixture, which adds even more sweetness to the topping. ◆ This tart serves about four to six.

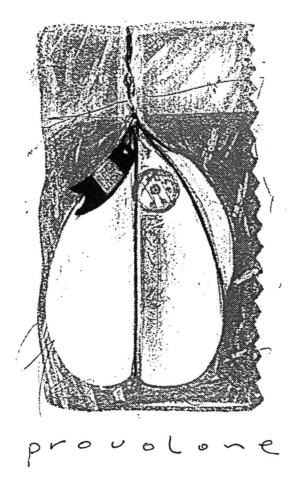

provolone

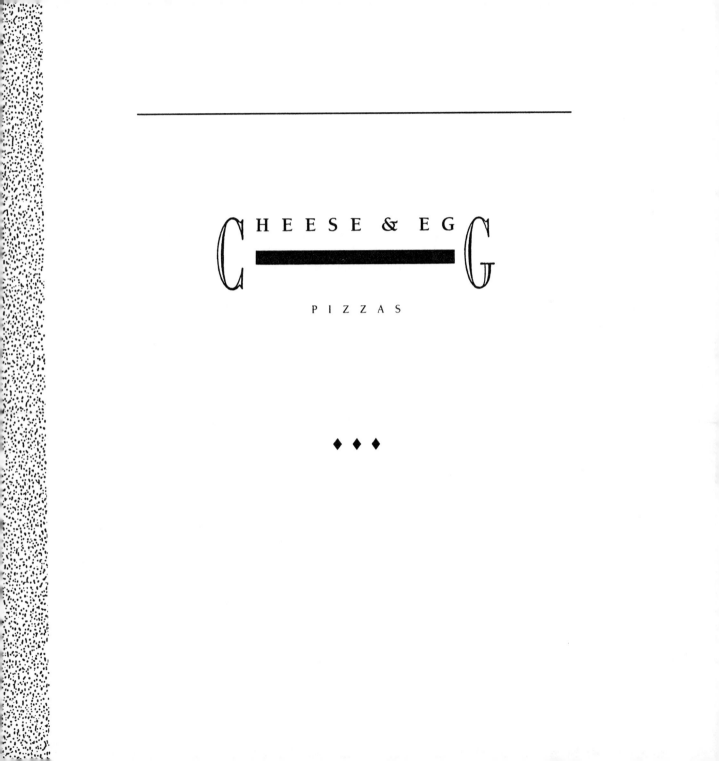

CHEESE & EGG

P I Z Z A S

◆ ◆ ◆

E ven though mozzarella is the cheese of choice for most pizzas, other cheeses can be used as long as they have good melting qualities, such as Cheddar, Monterey Jack, fontina, or goat.

♦ Here Cheddar cheese and bacon blend beautifully as a topping for pizza.

CHEDDAR BACON PIZZA

3 slices bacon, diced	½ cup grated mozzarella
Prepared dough, enough for	cheese
one 10-inch pizza	2 very thin slices red onion,
Olive oil	separated into rings
½ cup grated Cheddar	Salt
cheese	Freshly ground black pepper

LINE OVEN RACK with quarry tiles or pizza stone if using. Preheat oven to 500°F for 1 hour.

Sprinkle peel with cornmeal or flour, or lightly coat a black pizza pan with olive oil.

In a small skillet, cook bacon until just beginning to crisp; remove to a paper towel-lined plate to drain.

Hand stretch or roll out dough into a 10-inch circle and place on peel or pan. Brush dough lightly with olive oil to cover completely.

Spread the cheeses over dough, leaving a 1/2-inch border. Top with bacon and red onion. Lightly salt and add a few grindings of black pepper

Bake for 5 to 10 minutes, or until cheese is bubbly and crust is golden.

GOAT CHEESE AND SUN-DRIED TOMATO PIZZA

Prepared dough, enough for
  one 10-inch pizza
Oil from sun-dried tomatoes
4 ounces soft goat cheese,
  cut into 4 slices
2 large (whole) sun-dried
  tomatoes in oil, drained
  and coarsely shredded

¼ teaspoon dried thyme
Salt
Freshly ground black pepper
10 fresh basil leaves for
  garnish

LINE OVEN rack with quarry tiles or pizza stone if using. Preheat oven to 500°F for 1 hour.

Sprinkle peel with cornmeal or flour, or lightly coat a black pizza pan with olive or vegetable oil.

Hand stretch or roll dough into a 10-inch circle and place on peel or pan. Brush dough with 2 teaspoons sun-dried tomato oil to cover completely.

Arrange the cheese slices equally around dough, leaving a ½-inch border. Place shredded sun-dried tomatoes around cheese slices. Sprinkle with thyme, salt, and a few grindings of pepper. Drizzle ½ teaspoon sun-dried tomato oil over pizza.

Bake for 5 to 10 minutes, or until cheese is bubbly and lightly flecked with golden-brown spots.

Remove pizza from oven and garnish with basil leaves.

Goat cheese and sun-dried tomato enthusiasts are invariably crazy about this scrumptious and pretty pizza. ◆ It's one of my personal favorites, too.

classic combination of four cheeses with a trendy California touch – the addition of sun-dried tomatoes.

FOUR CHEESE PIZZA

Prepared dough, enough for one 10-inch pizza
Olive oil
½ cup grated provolone cheese
¼ cup crumbled Gorgonzola cheese
¼ cup grated mozzarella cheese

1 tablespoon freshly grated Romano cheese
Freshly ground black pepper
2 large (whole) sun-dried tomatoes, drained and finely chopped

LINE OVEN RACK with quarry tiles or pizza stone if using. Preheat oven to 500°F for 1 hour

Sprinkle peel with cornmeal or flour, or lightly coat a black pizza pan with olive oil.

Hand stretch or roll out dough into a 10-inch circle and place on peel or pan.

Brush dough lightly with oil to cover completely. Spread cheeses over dough, leaving a ½-inch border Add a few grindings of black pepper

Bake for 5 to 10 minutes, or until cheese is bubbly.

Remove pizza from oven and sprinkle with sun-dried tomatoes.

PROVOLONE PIZZA

Prepared dough, enough for
  one 10-inch pizza
Olive oil
½ cup No-Cook Tomato
  Sauce (see page 27)
½ cup grated provolone
  cheese
½ cup grated mozzarella
  cheese
½ teaspoon dried oregano
Salt
Freshly ground black pepper

LINE OVEN RACK with quarry tiles or pizza stone if using.
Preheat oven to 500°F for 1 hour.
   Sprinkle peel with cornmeal or flour, or lightly coat a
black pizza pan.
   Hand stretch or roll out dough into a 10-inch circle and
place on peel or pan. Brush dough lightly with oil to cover
completely.
   Spread tomato sauce over dough, leaving a ½-inch border.
Spread cheeses over sauce. Sprinkle with oregano. Salt
lightly and add a few grindings of pepper.
   Bake for 5 to 10 minutes, or until cheese is flecked with
golden-brown spots. Watch pizza carefully. Because there
are no toppings covering the cheese, this pizza browns
more quickly.

Don't let the simplicity of the ingredients fool you into bypassing this recipe — absolutely everyone who has taken part in my pizza-tasting experiments picks this as their favorite. ◆ No matter how delicious or different my other pizzas are, I think this epitomizes the quintessential pizza. ◆ Please use Italian provolone cheese for the best flavor.

lusty, exquisite pie — one of my favorites. ♦ *Serve with a robust red wine and a simple green salad*

MEDITERRANEAN PIZZA

Prepared dough, enough for one 10-inch pizza
Olive oil
¼ pound crumbled feta cheese
½ cup grated mozzarella cheese
1 ripe medium tomato (about ¼ pound), seeded and diced
1 medium garlic clove, finely chopped
8 Greek black olives (Kalamata), pitted and coarsely chopped
¼ teaspoon dried thyme
Salt
Freshly ground black pepper

LINE OVEN RACK with quarry tiles or pizza stone if using. Preheat oven to 500°F for 1 hour.

Sprinkle peel with cornmeal or flour, or lightly coat a black pizza pan with olive oil.

Hand stretch or roll out dough into a 10-inch circle and place on pan. Brush dough lightly with oil to cover completely.

Spread cheeses over dough, leaving a ½-inch border. Top with tomato, garlic, and olives. Sprinkle with thyme, salt, and pepper.

Bake for 5 to 10 minutes, or until cheese is bubbling and crust is golden

GORGONZOLA AND CARAMELIZED ONION PIZZA

2 tablespoons butter
1 large onion, thinly sliced
Prepared dough, enough for one 10-inch pizza
Olive oil
½ cup crumbled Gorgonzola cheese
½ cup grated mozzarella cheese
1 large garlic clove, thinly sliced
Freshly ground black pepper
2 tablespoons coarsely chopped fresh basil leaves

LINE OVEN RACK with quarry tiles or pizza stone if using. Preheat oven to 500°F for 1 hour.

Sprinkle peel with cornmeal or flour, or lightly coat a black pizza pan with olive oil.

In a heavy medium saucepan, melt butter. Add onion and cook on low heat for 25 to 30 minutes, or until very soft and caramelized. Set aside.

Hand stretch or roll out dough into a 10-inch circle and place on peel or pan. Just brush edges of dough lightly with oil to cover completely.

Spread onion mixture over dough, leaving a ½-inch border. Top onion mixture with cheeses, garlic, and a few grindings of pepper.

Bake for 5 to 10 minutes, or until crust is golden and cheese is flecked with golden-brown spots.

Remove pizza from oven and sprinkle with basil.

B*lue cheese lovers will be tempted by this happy marriage of pungent Gorgonzola and sweet braised onions. ◆ It's very rich, so serve in small wedges as an hors d'oeuvre.*

W—ho would have thought you could enjoy pizza for breakfast? Here's a pizza to serve for breakfast or brunch. It may be unconventional, but it really is very tasty. ◆ Be careful not to overcook the egg; the white should be set, but the yolk still runny. ◆ You must cook this pizza on a pan, because the egg would slide off while using the peel.

Bacon and Egg Pizza

3 slices bacon, diced
Prepared dough, enough for
  one 10-inch pizza
Olive oil
⅔ cup grated provolone
  cheese
1 large egg
1 ripe medium tomato
  (about ¼ pound), seeded
  and diced
Salt
Freshly ground black pepper
1 tablespoon freshly grated
  Parmesan cheese
2 tablespoons finely
  chopped fresh parsley

PREHEAT OVEN to 500°F for 1 hour.

Lightly coat a black pizza pan with olive oil.

In a small skillet, cook bacon until just crisp and remove to a paper towel-lined plate to drain.

Hand stretch or roll out dough into a 10-inch circle and place on pan. Brush dough lightly with oil to cover completely. Spread a little of the cheese over dough, leaving a ½-inch border. Shape the remaining cheese into a nest shape in the center of dough. Gently break the egg into the well; carefully top with bacon and tomato (don't break yolk) and lightly salt and add a generous grinding of black pepper. Sprinkle with Parmesan cheese.

Bake for 5 to 10 minutes, or until egg is set. Remove from oven, sprinkle with parsley, and serve immediately.

VEGETABLE & FRUIT

PIZZAS

◆ ◆ ◆

*D*eep-fried parsley fans will enjoy this interesting topping. ◆ Green and fresh-tasting, the parsley sort of "fries" and crisps while baking.

PARSLEY PIZZA

Prepared dough, enough for one 10-inch pizza
Olive oil
1 cup finely chopped fresh parsley

1 large garlic clove, finely chopped
Salt
Freshly ground black pepper
1 tablespoon freshly grated Parmesan cheese

LINE OVEN RACK with quarry tiles or pizza stone if using. Preheat oven to 500°F for 1 hour.

Sprinkle peel with cornmeal or flour, or lightly coat a black pizza pan with olive oil.

Hand stretch or roll out dough into a 10-inch circle and place on peel or pan. Brush dough lightly with oil to cover completely.

Spread parsley over dough, leaving a ½-inch border. Top with garlic. Drizzle with 2 teaspoons oil; lightly salt, and add a few grindings of pepper.

Bake for 5 to 10 minutes, or until crust is golden.

Remove pizza from oven and sprinkle with Parmesan cheese.

SPINACH CHIFFONADE AND BACON PIZZA

3 slices bacon, diced
Prepared dough, enough for one 10-inch pizza
Olive oil
1 cup grated mozzarella cheese

1 cup shredded spinach leaves (preferably baby spinach)
Salt
Freshly ground black pepper
Freshly grated nutmeg

LINE OVEN RACK with quarry tiles or pizza stone if using. Preheat oven to 500°F for 1 hour.

Sprinkle peel with cornmeal or flour, or lightly coat a black pizza pan with olive oil.

In a small skillet, cook bacon until just crisp and remove to a paper towel-lined plate to drain.

Hand stretch or roll out dough into a 10-inch circle and place on peel or pan. Brush dough lightly with oil to cover completely

Spread cheese over dough, leaving a ½-inch border. Spread spinach over cheese and top with bacon. Lightly salt and add a few grindings of pepper.

Bake for 5 to 10 minutes, or until crust is golden.

Remove from oven and grate a little nutmeg over pizza.

Other greens, such as beet greens or chicory, may be used instead of spinach.
♦ This is a rustic, satisfying pizza.

spatula and pan

ith its combination of fresh basil, garlic, olive oil, pine nuts, and Parmesan or Romano cheese, pesto not only graces pasta, but is also a fragrant topping for pizza. ◆ Slice in thin wedges and serve as an appetizer; it is a bit too rich for a single serving. ◆ As a variation, omit pine nuts and top pesto with diced tomatoes or cooked shrimp.

PESTO PIZZA

Prepared dough, enough for one 10-inch pizza
⅓ cup Pesto Sauce (see page 29)
1 tablespoon lightly toasted pine nuts*

Salt
Freshly ground black pepper
1 tablespoon freshly grated Parmesan cheese

LINE OVEN RACK with quarry tiles or pizza stone if using. Preheat oven to 500°F for 1 hour.

Sprinkle peel with cornmeal or flour, or lightly coat a black pizza pan with olive oil.

Hand stretch or roll out dough into a 10-inch circle and place on peel or pan.

Spread pesto sauce over dough, leaving a ½-inch border. Brush edges of dough lightly with oil. Sprinkle pine nuts over sauce. Lightly salt and add a few grindings of black pepper.

Bake for 5 to 10 minutes, or until crust is golden. The dough might bubble up in the center because the topping isn't heavy; I like this rustic look, but if you prefer a more refined appearance, just jab it with the sharp point of a knife to deflate bubbles while the pizza is baking.

Remove pizza from oven and sprinkle with Parmesan cheese.

*Note: Spread pine nuts in an unoiled, heavy skillet. Place on moderate heat and stir occasionally until golden. Be careful not to overbrown.

Spring Pizza

Prepared dough, enough for one 10-inch pizza
Olive oil
4 very thin asparagus spears, blanched and dried well
⅛ cup fresh fiddleheads, blanched and squeezed dry to remove moisture
4 very thin rings sweet red pepper
¼ cup coarsely chopped fresh parsley
¼ teaspoon dried tarragon
Salt
Freshly ground black pepper
1 tablespoon freshly grated Parmesan cheese

LINE OVEN RACK with quarry tiles or pizza stone if using. Preheat oven to 500°F for 1 hour. Sprinkle peel with cornmeal or flour, or lightly coat a black pizza pan with olive oil.

Hand stretch or roll out dough into a 10-inch circle and place on pan. Brush dough lightly with oil to cover completely

Arrange asparagus on dough in spoke pattern. Top with fiddleheads, red pepper, parsley, tarragon, salt, and a few grindings of pepper. Drizzle with 1 teaspoon oil.

Bake for 5 to 10 minutes, or until crust is golden.

Remove pizza from oven and sprinkle with Parmesan cheese.

C *elebrate the first asparagus and fiddleheads of spring by making this pizza.* ♦ *It's light and delightful.*

*resh, light, and very
sophisticated.*

FENNEL PIZZA

Olive oil
1 medium fennel bulb, top
   removed, thinly sliced
   (reserve 5 or 6 fronds)
1 medium onion, thinly
   sliced
2 large garlic cloves,
   chopped

Prepared dough, enough for
   one 10-inch pizza
Salt
Freshly ground black pepper
2 tablespoons freshly grated
   Parmesan cheese

LINE OVEN RACK with quarry tiles or pizza stone if using. Preheat oven to 500°F for 1 hour.

Sprinkle peel with cornmeal or flour, or lightly coat a black pizza pan with olive oil.

In a medium skillet, heat 2 tablespoons olive oil. Add fennel, onion, and garlic and cook for 30 minutes on low heat, until soft but not brown. Set aside.

Hand stretch or roll out dough into a 10-inch circle and place on peel or pan.

Just brush edges of dough lightly with oil.

Spread fennel mixture over dough, leaving a ½-inch border. Top with fennel fronds, salt, and a few grindings of pepper.

Bake for 5 to 10 minutes, or until crust is golden.

Remove pizza from oven and sprinkle with cheese.

RED ONION AND PARMESAN PIZZA

Prepared dough, enough for one 10-inch pizza	½ teaspoon dried basil or oregano
Olive oil	Salt
2 tablespoons freshly grated Parmesan cheese	Freshly ground black pepper
2 very thin slices red onion, separated into rings	

LINE OVEN RACK with quarry tiles or pizza stone if using. Preheat oven to 500°F for 1 hour.

Sprinkle peel with cornmeal or flour, or lightly coat a black pizza pan with olive oil.

Hand stretch or roll out dough into a 10-inch circle and place on peel or pan. Brush dough lightly with oil to cover completely.

Sprinkle cheese over dough, leaving a ½-inch border. Arrange onion slices on top. Sprinkle with basil; lightly salt, and add a few grindings of pepper. Drizzle with 1 teaspoon oil.

Bake for 5 minutes, or until crust is golden. Serve with Spicy Oil (see page 30).

*S*weet red onions and Parmesan cheese — a simple yet sublime topping. ◆ Because the topping is light, the crust will puff up through the center. If that bothers you, just open the oven door and jab the bubbles with a very sharp knife to deflate them. ◆ It is best to grate the Parmesan by hand, because the food processor grates it into little balls that don't melt properly

Ratatouille is an aromatic
Provençal eggplant stew best
made when summer's vege-
tables are at their peak. It
makes a delicious topping for pizza.
◆ Serve leftover ratatouille as a cold
side dish to accompany grilled meats
or fish.

RATATOUILLE PIZZA

Prepared dough, enough for
  one 10-inch pizza
Olive oil
1 cup ratatouille
  (see page 28)
Salt
Freshly ground black pepper

2 tablespoons freshly grated
  Parmesan cheese
1 tablespoon finely chopped
  fresh parsley
1 tablespoon shredded
  fresh basil leaves

LINE OVEN RACK with quarry tiles or pizza stone if using.
Preheat oven to 500°F for 1 hour.

Sprinkle peel with cornmeal or flour, or lightly coat a
black pizza pan with olive oil.

Hand stretch or roll out dough into a 10-inch circle and
place on peel or pan. Brush dough lightly with oil to cover
completely.

Spread ratatouille over dough, leaving a ½-inch border.
Lightly salt and add a few grindings of pepper.

Bake for 5 to 10 minutes, or until crust is golden.

Remove pizza from oven and sprinkle with Parmesan
cheese, parsley, and basil.

WILD MUSHROOM PIZZA

Prepared dough, enough for
one 10-inch pizza
Olive oil
5 ounces fresh wild
mushrooms, stems
removed
¼ teaspoon dried thyme
¼ teaspoon dried basil
Freshly ground black pepper
1 cup grated mozzarella
cheese
Salt
1 tablespoon freshly grated
Parmesan cheese
1 tablespoon finely chopped
fresh parsley

LINE OVEN RACK with quarry tiles or pizza stone if using. Preheat oven to 500°F for 1 hour.

Sprinkle peel with cornmeal or flour, or lightly coat a black pizza pan with olive oil.

Hand stretch or roll out dough into a 10-inch circle and place on peel or pan. Brush dough lightly with oil to cover completely.

In a bowl, toss mushrooms, 2 tablespoons olive oil, thyme, basil, and pepper. Spread mushroom mixture and mozzarella cheese over dough, leaving a ½-inch border. Lightly salt.

Bake for 5 to 10 minutes, or until crust is golden.

Remove pizza from oven and sprinkle with Parmesan cheese and parsley.

Woodsy-flavored and wonderful. ◆ *You may use any combination of fresh wild mushrooms (shiitake, porcini, chanterelles, morels) or just one variety — whatever you can forage at your local fancy greengrocer, or in the woods if you are an expert mycologist.*

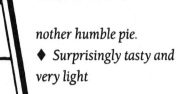

nother humble pie.
♦ *Surprisingly tasty and very light*

ZUCCHINI PIZZA

Olive oil
1 medium zucchini, sliced
1 small onion, thinly sliced
2 large garlic cloves, chopped
½ cup coarsely chopped fresh parsley
¼ cup coarsely chopped fresh basil leaves

Prepared dough, enough for one 10-inch pizza
1 cup grated mozzarella cheese
1 ripe medium tomato (about ¼ pound), seeded and diced
Salt
Freshly ground black pepper

LINE OVEN RACK with quarry tiles or pizza stone if using. Preheat oven to 500°F for 1 hour.

Sprinkle peel with cornmeal or flour; or lightly coat a black pizza pan with olive oil.

In a heavy medium skillet, heat 2 tablespoons oil. Add zucchini, onion, garlic, parsley, and basil and cook for 4 minutes, or until zucchini is crisp-tender. Set aside.

Hand stretch or roll out dough into a 10-inch circle and place on peel or pan. Brush dough lightly with oil to cover completely.

Spread cheese over dough, leaving a ½-inch border. Spread zucchini mixture over cheese. Top with tomato; lightly salt, and add a few grindings of pepper.

Bake for 5 to 10 minutes, or until crust is golden.

ROASTED GARLIC, EGGPLANT, AND FRESH BASIL PIZZA

1 Japanese eggplant
(⅓ pound), unpeeled and
cut lengthwise into ¼-inch
slices
Olive oil
1 large whole head garlic
(about 18 cloves), cloves
peeled and left whole
Prepared dough, enough for
one 10-inch pizza

½ cup No-Cook Tomato
Sauce (see page 27)
1 cup grated mozzarella
cheese
½ teaspoon dried oregano
Salt
Freshly ground black pepper
1 tablespoon chopped fresh
basil or mint leaves

BRUSH EGGPLANT on both sides with olive oil and place on broiler pan. Broil until lightly browned, about 5 minutes on each side. Remove to a plate and set aside.

Preheat oven to 500°F for 1 hour.

In a small heavy skillet, on medium-low heat, cook garlic cloves in 2 tablespoons olive oil until tender and very lightly colored, about 15 to 20 minutes. Be careful not to allow the cloves to brown, or they will be bitter. Drain excess oil and set aside.

Lightly coat a black pizza pan with olive oil.

Hand stretch or roll out dough into a 10-inch circle and place on pan. Brush dough lightly with oil to cover completely.

Spread tomato sauce over dough, leaving a ½-inch border. Sprinkle cheese over sauce. Arrange eggplant slices in a spoke pattern with the square ends in the center. Scatter braised garlic over top. Sprinkle with oregano; lightly salt, and add a few grindings of pepper.

Bake for 5 to 10 minutes, or until crust is golden and cheese is bubbling.

Remove pizza from oven and sprinkle with basil.

An enticing, Mediterranean-inspired topping. ◆ Do not be alarmed by the number of whole garlic cloves; they are first slowly braised until they become soft and mellow. ◆ Do choose fresh, plump garlic heads for the best results.

lways a hit with garlic and hot pepper fanatics. ♦ The hot pickled pepper rings are available in most super-markets and in Italian food shops. ♦ You may also top the pizza with diced and cooked bacon as a variation.

HOT PICKLED PEPPERS AND GARLIC PIZZA

Prepared dough, enough for
  one 10-inch pizza
Olive oil
½ cup No-Cook Tomato
  Sauce (see page 27)
1 cup grated mozzarella
  cheese

1 to 2 tablespoons pickled
  hot pepper rings, drained
2 large garlic cloves, finely
  chopped
½ teaspoon dried oregano
Salt

LINE OVEN RACK with quarry tiles or pizza stone if using. Preheat oven to 500°F for 1 hour.

Sprinkle peel with cornmeal or flour, or lightly coat a black pizza pan with olive oil.

Hand stretch or roll out dough into a 10-inch circle and place on peel or pan. Brush dough lightly with oil to cover completely.

Spread tomato sauce over dough, leaving a ½-inch border. Spread cheese over sauce. Top with hot peppers and garlic. Sprinkle with oregano and a little salt.

Bake for 5 to 10 minutes, or until cheese is flecked with golden-brown spots and crust is golden.

ROASTED RED PEPPER PIZZA

1 large sweet red pepper, roasted (see page 72)
Prepared Thin and Crispy dough, enough for one 10-inch pizza
Olive oil
2 ounces fresh mozzarella or provolone cheese, sliced

4 very thin rings sweet yellow pepper
1 medium garlic clove, finely chopped
Salt
Freshly ground black pepper
8 large fresh basil leaves

LINE OVEN RACK with quarry tiles or pizza stone if using. Preheat oven to 500°F for 1 hour.

Sprinkle peel with cornmeal or flour, or lightly coat a black pizza pan with olive oil.

In a food processor, puree roasted red pepper.

Hand stretch or roll out dough into a 10-inch circle and place on peel or pan. Brush dough lightly with oil to completely cover. Spread red pepper puree over dough, leaving a ½-inch border. Top with mozzarella and yellow pepper slices. Sprinkle with garlic. Salt lightly and add a few grindings of pepper.

Bake for 5 to 10 minutes or until cheese is bubbly and crust is golden. Remove from oven and garnish with basil leaves.

A *beguiling array of summer flavors and vivid colors — roasted red pepper puree topped with yellow peppers, basil leaves, and fresh mozzarella — makes an irresistible pizza topping.*
♦ *Absolutely delicious!*

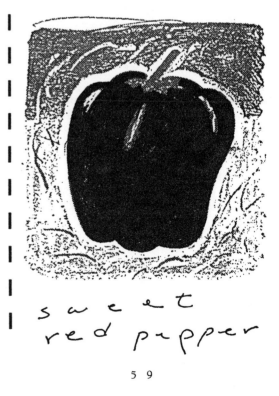

sweet red pepper

eminiscent of my very first pizza. ◆ The combination is as satisfying now as it was then

MUSHROOM, RED AND GREEN PEPPER PIZZA

Prepared dough, enough for one 10-inch pizza
Olive oil
½ cup No-Cook Tomato Sauce (see page 27)
1 cup grated provolone cheese
1 tablespoon freshly grated Parmesan cheese

5 ounces fresh mushrooms, thinly sliced
2 thin rings sweet red pepper
2 thin rings sweet green pepper
Salt
Freshly ground black pepper

LINE OVEN RACK with quarry tiles or pizza stone if using. Preheat oven to 500°F for 1 hour.

Sprinkle peel with cornmeal or flour, or lightly coat a black pizza pan with olive oil.

Hand stretch or roll out dough into a 10-inch circle and place on peel or pan. Brush dough lightly with oil to cover completely.

Spread tomato sauce over dough, leaving a ½-inch border. Spread cheeses over sauce. Top with mushrooms and peppers. Lightly salt and add a few grindings of pepper.

Bake for 5 to 10 minutes, or until crust is golden and cheese is bubbling.

THREE PEPPER PIZZA

Olive oil
3 large garlic cloves, chopped
1 small sweet red pepper, seeded and cut into julienne
½ small sweet green pepper, seeded and cut into julienne
½ small sweet yellow pepper, seeded and cut into julienne
1 medium onion, thinly sliced
1 teaspoon dried basil or oregano
Salt
Freshly ground black pepper
Prepared dough, enough for one 10-inch pizza
10 Greek black olives (Kalamata), unpitted

LINE OVEN RACK with quarry tiles or pizza stone if using. Preheat oven to 500°F for 1 hour.

Sprinkle peel with cornmeal or flour, or lightly coat a black pizza pan with olive oil.

In a heavy medium skillet, heat 2 tablespoons olive oil. Add garlic, peppers, onion, basil, salt, and pepper. Cook over low heat for 25 to 30 minutes, or until very soft but not brown.

Hand stretch or roll out dough into a 10-inch circle and place on peel or pan. Just brush edges of dough with oil.

Spread pepper mixture over dough, leaving a ½-inch border. Top with olives.

Bake for 5 to 10 minutes, or until crust is golden.

resh sweet peppers in wonderful shades of green, red, and yellow are braised until soft and richly flavored before topping the pizza. ◆ A surprise to many people who think that all pizzas must have cheese and tomato sauce — this has neither! ◆ This delectable, low-cholesterol pizza is definitely not for dieters only.

his savory pizza has no tomatoes and very little cheese, making it low-calorie and low-cholesterol. ◆ It needs a little extra attention to ensure that the crust doesn't get soggy. Do not wash the mushrooms; just wipe them with a paper towel to remove the dirt, or the moisture will seep out while the pizza is cooking. It is also important to squeeze moisture out of the blanched broccoli; then dry well with a clean towel. ◆ As a variation you can add a little browned Italian sausage.

BROCCOLI, RED PEPPER, AND MUSHROOM PIZZA

Prepared dough, enough for one 10-inch pizza
Olive oil
¼ pound broccoli florets, blanched and chopped
2 ounces fresh mushrooms, sliced (about 1 cup)
2 tablespoons finely chopped fresh parsley
4 very thin rings sweet red pepper
1 large garlic clove, finely chopped
1 tablespoon freshly grated Parmesan cheese

PREHEAT OVEN to 500°F for 1 hour. Lightly coat a black pizza pan with olive oil.

Hand stretch or roll out dough into a 10-inch circle and place on pan. Brush dough lightly with oil to cover completely.

Place broccoli, mushrooms, parsley, red pepper, and garlic over dough, leaving a ½-inch border. Drizzle with 1 teaspoon olive oil.

Bake for 5 to 10 minutes, or until crust is golden.

Remove pizza from oven and sprinkle with Parmesan cheese. Serve with Spicy Oil (see page 30).

TEX-MEX PIZZA

Prepared dough, enough for
   one 10-inch pizza
Olive oil
1 ripe large tomato, seeded
   and diced
1 large jalapeño pepper,
   roasted and chopped*
2 green onions, chopped
1 large garlic clove, chopped

1 cup grated Cheddar cheese
1 tablespoon freshly grated
   Parmesan cheese
Salt
Freshly ground black pepper
½ ripe avocado, cubed
¼ cup sour cream
2 tablespoons chopped
   fresh coriander

Do try this one. It has become a favorite of everyone I have served it to. ◆ The juxtaposition of the cold ingredients on top of the hot crust is sensational.

LINE OVEN RACK with quarry tiles or pizza stone if using. Preheat oven to 500°F for 1 hour.

Hand stretch or roll out dough into a 10-inch circle and place on peel or pan. Brush dough lightly with oil to cover completely.

Spread tomatoes over dough, leaving a ½-inch border. Top with jalapēno, green onions, and garlic. Spread Cheddar cheese over vegetables; sprinkle with Parmesan cheese. Lightly salt and add a few grindings of black pepper.

Bake for 5 to 10 minutes, or until cheese is bubbly and crust is golden.

Remove pizza from oven and top with avocado, a dollop of sour cream, and coriander. Pass extra sour cream.

*Note: To roast jalapeño, place on a cake rack over an electric burner on high heat or spear with a skewer and place over gas flame on stove. Cook until charred and blistered on all sides. Be careful not to burn too deeply, or you will overcook peppers. Remove stems, peel off skins, and remove seeds.

Although I'm not normally enamored of fruit on pizza, one day I happened to have some apples and Brie in the refrigerator and decided to be daring.

♦ The result was intriguing and really delicious; the only problem I had was trying to figure out if it was a light lunch or a dessert pizza.

APPLE AND BRIE PIZZA

Prepared dough, enough for one 10-inch pizza
Olive oil
1 large McIntosh apple, unpeeled, cored, and thinly sliced
Lemon juice
5 ounces Brie cheese (rind removed), cut into small pieces
1 teaspoon butter
Freshly grated nutmeg

LINE OVEN RACK with quarry tiles or pizza stone if using. Preheat oven to 500°F for 1 hour.

Sprinkle peel with cornmeal or flour, or lightly coat a black pizza pan with olive oil.

Hand stretch or roll out dough into a 10-inch circle and place on peel or pan. Brush dough lightly with oil to cover completely.

Toss apple slices with a little lemon juice to prevent darkening. Arrange slices in concentric circles over dough, leaving a ½-inch border. Top with Brie and dot with butter.

Bake for 5 minutes, or until crust and apples are golden. Watch carefully so apples don't overcook.

Remove pizza from oven and grate a little nutmeg over apples.

TAPENADE PIZZA

1 cup black olives (Niçoise or Kalamata), pitted
3 anchovy fillets, drained
1 tablespoon capers, drained
Olive oil

Prepared dough, enough for one 10-inch pizza
1 cup grated mozzarella cheese
1 heaping teaspoon grated orange zest

LINE OVEN RACK with quarry tiles or pizza stone if using. Preheat oven to 500°F for 1 hour.

To make tapenade, in a food processor, process olives, anchovies, capers, and 2 teaspoons olive oil until mixture becomes a rough paste.

Sprinkle peel with cornmeal or flour, or lightly coat a black pizza pan with olive oil.

Hand stretch or roll out dough into a 10-inch circle and place on peel or pan. Brush dough lightly with oil to cover completely.

Spread ⅓ cup tapenade over dough, leaving a ½-inch border. Spread cheese over tapenade. Sprinkle with orange zest. Bake for 5 to 10 minutes, or until crust is golden.

*G*utsy and pungent!
◆ *Tapenade is a specialty of Provence — a spread or paste of capers, olives, anchovies, and olive oil.* ◆ *Serve this pizza in small wedges as an appetizer with cocktails or before dinner.*
◆ *Leftover tapenade is wonderful as a spread for crackers; it can also be thinned with olive oil and tossed with pasta.*

Unusual and assertive. ♦ It pleases my palate, but I must warn you — it is not for the timid!

GREEN OLIVE PIZZA

½ cup pimiento-stuffed olives
Prepared dough, enough for one 10-inch pizza
Olive oil

½ cup No-Cook Tomato Sauce (see page 27)
1 cup grated mozzarella cheese
½ teaspoon dried oregano
Freshly ground black pepper

LINE OVEN RACK with quarry tiles or pizza stone if using. Preheat oven to 500°F for 1 hour.

In a food processor, process olives until finely chopped. Do not overprocess into a paste.

Sprinkle peel with cornmeal or flour, or lightly coat a black pizza pan with olive oil.

Hand stretch or roll out dough into a 10-inch circle and place on peel or pan. Brush dough lightly with oil to cover completely.

Spread tomato sauce over dough, leaving a ½-inch border. Spread ½ cup cheese over tomato sauce. Top with olives; spread remaining cheese over olives, and sprinkle with oregano and a few grindings of pepper. (Do not salt because the olives are salty.)

Bake for 5 to 10 minutes, or until crust is golden and cheese is bubbling.

PUTTANESCA PIZZA

Prepared dough, enough for
   one 10-inch pizza
Olive oil
½ teaspoon dried oregano
½ cup grated mozzarella
   cheese
½ cup grated provolone
   cheese
1 large garlic clove,
   finely chopped

10 Greek black olives
   (Kalamata), pitted and
   coarsely chopped
2 tablespoons capers, drained
1 very thin slice red onion,
   separated into rings
1 medium ripe tomato
   (about ¼ pound), seeded
   and diced
Salt
Freshly ground black pepper

LINE OVEN RACK with quarry tiles or pizza stone if using. Preheat oven to 500°F for 1 hour.

Sprinkle peel with cornmeal or flour, or lightly coat a black pizza pan with olive oil.

Hand stretch or roll out dough into a 10-inch circle and place on peel or pan. Brush dough lightly with oil to cover completely.

Sprinkle dough with oregano. Spread cheeses over dough, leaving a ½-inch border. Top with garlic, olives, capers, onions, and tomato. Lightly salt and add a few grindings of pepper

Bake for 5 to 10 minutes, or until cheese is flecked with brown and crust is golden.

*T*hese same pungent flavorings — lots of garlic, tomatoes, black olives, and capers — go into the famous Italian pasta sauce named for the ladies of the evening. But they also make a wonderful topping for pizza. ◆ The combination isn't subtle, but that is why I love it so much. ◆ As a variation, add a few sliced marinated artichoke hearts.

crab

SEAFOOD & FISH

PIZZAS

◆ ◆ ◆

Most people either love or hate anchovies. ◆ If you love them, this pizza is for you. Even if you don't think you like anchovies, why not be daring and try this? Chances are one taste will make you change your mind.

ANCHOVY, RED PEPPER, AND ONION PIZZA

Prepared dough, enough for one 10-inch pizza
Olive oil
½ cup No-Cook Tomato Sauce (see page 27)
½ cup grated provolone cheese
½ cup grated mozzarella cheese
8 anchovy fillets, drained
4 very thin rings sweet red pepper
1 very thin slice red onion, separated into rings
¼ teaspoon dried thyme
¼ teaspoon dried oregano
Freshly ground black pepper

LINE OVEN RACK with quarry tiles or pizza stone if using. Preheat oven to 500°F for 1 hour.

Sprinkle peel with cornmeal or flour, or lightly coat a black pizza pan with olive oil.

Hand stretch or roll out dough into a 10-inch circle and place on peel or pan. Brush dough lightly with oil to cover completely.

Spread tomato sauce over dough, leaving a ½-inch border. Spread cheeses over sauce. Arrange anchovies in a spoke pattern; top with red pepper and onion slices. Sprinkle with thyme, oregano, and a few grindings of pepper. (Do not salt; the anchovies are salty enough.)

Bake for 5 to 10 minutes, or until cheese is flecked with golden-brown spots and crust is golden.

SMOKED OYSTER AND RED ONION PIZZA

Prepared dough, enough for
one 10-inch pizza
Olive oil
½ teaspoon dried oregano
1 cup grated mozzarella
cheese
1 large garlic clove
finely chopped

1 to 2 very thin slices red
onion, separated into rings
3½-ounce (104-g) can
smoked oysters, drained
Salt
Freshly ground black pepper

LINE OVEN RACK with quarry tiles or pizza stone if using.
Preheat oven to 500°F for 1 hour.

Sprinkle peel with cornmeal or flour, or lightly coat a black
pizza pan with olive oil.

Hand stretch or roll out dough into a 10-inch circle and
place on peel or pan Brush dough lightly with oil to cover
completely.

Sprinkle dough with oregano. Spread cheese over dough,
leaving a ½-inch border. Top with garlic, onion, and oysters.
Lightly salt and add a few grindings of black pepper.

Bake for 5 to 10 minutes, or until cheese is bubbly and
crust is golden

One day when I was peering into my cupboard for inspiration, I found some smoked oysters and wondered, why not? ◆ So I experimented, and the results were surprisingly good — the oysters infused the topping with a rich, smoky flavor

I only recently discovered how wonderful canned tuna can be in a pasta sauce, when it is combined with zesty capers and other Mediterranean flavorings. It is equally fabulous as a topping for pizza. ♦ As a variation I often add several Kalamata olives.

TUNA, ROASTED RED PEPPERS, AND CAPER PIZZA

Prepared dough, enough for one 10-inch pizza
Olive oil
1 cup grated mozzarella cheese
6½-ounce (184-g) can chunk light or solid white (not flaked) tuna, drained
1 medium roasted sweet red pepper*
2 tablespoons capers, drained
Salt
Freshly ground black pepper
2 tablespoons freshly grated Parmesan cheese

LINE OVEN RACK with quarry tiles or pizza stone if using. Preheat oven to 500°F for 1 hour.

Sprinkle peel with cornmeal or flour, or lightly coat a black pizza pan with olive oil.

Hand stretch or roll out dough into a 10-inch circle and place on peel or pan. Brush dough lightly with oil to cover completely.

Spread mozzarella over dough, leaving a ½-inch border. Top with tuna chunks, red pepper, and capers. Lightly salt and add a few grindings of pepper. Drizzle with 1 teaspoon oil.

Bake for 5 to 10 minutes, or until crust is golden.

Remove pizza from oven and sprinkle with Parmesan cheese. Serve with Spicy Oil (see page 30).

*Note: To roast red peppers, place whole peppers on baking sheet. Broil, turning frequently, for about 20 minutes, or until skin is blackened. Let stand until room temperature; peel, halve, and remove seeds. Slice into thick julienne.

SMOKED SALMON AND CAVIAR PIZZA

Prepared dough, enough for one 10-inch pizza
Olive oil
⅓ cup sour cream
3 ounces best-quality smoked salmon, cut into thick julienne

2 to 3 tablespoons salmon caviar
2 tablespoons chopped fresh chives

LINE OVEN RACK with quarry tiles or pizza stone if using. Preheat oven to 500°F for 1 hour.

Sprinkle peel with cornmeal or flour, or lightly coat a black pizza pan with olive oil.

Hand stretch or roll out dough into a 10-inch circle. With the tines of a fork, prick dough all over (except border) so that crust doesn't bubble up while cooking. Brush dough lightly with oil to cover completely.

Bake for 5 minutes, or until crust is golden.

Remove crust from oven and spread with sour cream, leaving a ½-inch border. Arrange salmon over sour cream and add a dollop or two of caviar in the center. Garnish with chives.

Ultimate bliss! Here the pizza crust is baked in the oven "nude" and then the toppings — smoked salmon, sour cream, chives, and caviar — are added after the crust has been removed from the oven. ◆ This makes a lovely appetizer pizza when cut in small wedges, but smoked salmon and caviar lovers like myself have been known to devour the whole thing in a matter of minutes. ◆ Salmon caviar is very perishable and should be bought frozen or just thawed and used as soon as possible.

This elegant pizza requires shrimp that are either fresh or frozen in their shells. ◆ Do not use the frozen, shelled bagged variety; they are watery and flavorless. Buy the shrimp at a quality fish store. ◆ This is a weight-watcher's special, because there is very little cheese.

SHRIMP, BRAISED LEEK, AND GARLIC PIZZA

Olive oil
1 to 2 leeks, white part only, chopped (about 2 cups)
6 large garlic cloves, peeled and left whole
Prepared dough, enough for one 10-inch pizza
½ pound medium shrimp, peeled, deveined, and cooked until just pink
1 ripe medium tomato (about ¼ pound), seeded and diced
½ teaspoon dried basil or oregano
Salt
Freshly ground black pepper
1 tablespoon freshly grated Parmesan cheese

LINE OVEN RACK with quarry tiles or pizza stone if using. Preheat oven to 500°F for 1 hour.

Sprinkle peel with cornmeal or flour, or lightly coat a black pizza pan with olive oil.

In a medium skillet, heat 2 tablespoons olive oil. Add leeks and garlic and cook on low heat for 20 minutes, or until garlic is soft but not brown. Set aside.

Hand stretch or roll out dough into a 10-inch circle and place on peel or pan. Just brush edges of dough lightly with oil.

Spread leek-garlic mixture over dough, leaving a ½-inch border. Place shrimp and tomato over leek mixture. Sprinkle with basil, salt, and several grindings of pepper.

Bake for 5 to 10 minutes, or until crust is golden.

Remove pizza from oven and sprinkle with Parmesan cheese.

SHRIMP AND FETA CHEESE PIZZA

Prepared dough, enough for
   one 10-inch pizza
Olive oil
½ cup No-Cook Tomato
   Sauce (see page 27)
½ cup grated mozzarella
   cheese
¼ pound feta cheese,
   crumbled

½ pound medium shrimp,
   shelled, deveined, and
   cooked
8 Greek black olives
   (Kalamata), unpitted
1 very thin slice red onion,
   separated into rings
½ teaspoon coarsely
   chopped fresh rosemary
Salt
Freshly ground black pepper

LINE OVEN RACK with quarry tiles or pizza stone if using. Preheat oven to 500°F for 1 hour.

Sprinkle peel with cornmeal or flour, or lightly coat a black pizza pan with olive oil.

Hand stretch or roll out dough into a 10-inch circle and place on peel or pan. Brush dough lightly with oil to cover completely.

Spread tomato sauce over dough, leaving a ½-inch border. Spread cheeses over sauce. Top with shrimp, olives, onion, and rosemary. Salt lightly and add a few grindings of pepper.

Bake for 5 to 10 minutes, or until cheese is bubbly and crust is golden. Serve with Spicy Oil (see page 30).

A pizza with Greek overtones. ◆ I love the combination of shrimp with feta cheese, black olives, and rosemary.

W orthy of the freshest crab meat you can buy. ♦ Frozen or canned just doesn't have the concentrated seafood flavor necessary for this delicate topping.

CRAB PIZZA

Prepared dough, enough for
  one 10-inch pizza
Olive oil
1 cup fresh crab meat
1 large garlic clove,
  finely chopped
¼ cup finely chopped
  fresh parsley
1 tablespoon freshly grated
  Parmesan cheese
Salt
Freshly ground black pepper

LINE OVEN RACK with quarry tiles or pizza stone if using. Preheat oven to 500°F for 1 hour.

Sprinkle peel with cornmeal or flour, or lightly coat a black pizza pan with olive oil.

Hand stretch or roll out dough into a 10-inch circle and place on peel or pan. Brush dough lightly with oil to cover completely.

Top dough with crab meat, garlic, parsley, and Parmesan cheese, leaving a ½-inch border. Lightly salt and add a few grindings of black pepper. Drizzle with 2 teaspoons oil.

Bake for 5 minutes, or until crust is golden. Do not overcook or the crab will dry out.

SEAFOOD PIZZA

Olive oil
½ pound cleaned squid, cut into rings
¼ pound shrimp, peeled and deveined
10 to 12 mussels, shucked
Prepared dough, enough for one 10-inch pizza
1 large garlic clove, finely chopped

1 ripe medium tomato (about ¼ pound), seeded and diced
1 tablespoon freshly grated Parmesan cheese
¼ teaspoon dried thyme
Salt
Freshly ground black pepper
1 tablespoon finely chopped fresh parsley
1 teaspoon grated lemon zest

LINE OVEN RACK with quarry tiles or pizza stone if using. Preheat oven to 500°F for 1 hour.

Sprinkle peel with cornmeal or flour, or lightly coat a black pizza pan with olive oil.

In a heavy medium skillet, heat 2 tablespoons oil. Cook squid, shrimp, and mussels for 1 to 2 minutes, or until squid turns opaque. Do not overcook; it is best that the seafood be undercooked. Set aside.

Hand stretch or roll out dough into a 10-inch circle and place on peel or pan. Just brush edges of dough lightly with oil.

Spread seafood mixture over dough, leaving a ½-inch border. Top with garlic and tomato. Sprinkle with cheese, thyme, salt, and a few grindings of pepper.

Bake for 5 to 10 minutes, or until crust is golden.

Remove from oven and sprinkle with parsley and lemon zest.

S eafoodies will enjoy this piquant topping.
♦ Substitute or combine your own favorite seafood. Try fresh sardines, clams, or octopus (sautéed in olive oil first) — even oysters.

mussels

A rustic and ancient pizza. It is low-cholesterol, light, and delicious. ◆ You may add grated Parmesan cheese at the table, although it is not traditional to serve cheese with this pizza. ◆ If you are lucky enough to have access to fresh littleneck clams, by all means substitute fresh shucked clams for the canned.

RED CLAM PIZZA

Prepared dough, enough for
  one 10-inch pizza
Olive oil
½ cup No-Cook Tomato
  Sauce (see page 27)

½ cup canned baby clams,
  drained (reserve
  2 teaspoons clam juice)
Salt
Freshly ground black pepper
½ teaspoon dried oregano

LINE OVEN RACK with quarry tiles or pizza stone if using. Preheat oven to 500°F for 1 hour.

Sprinkle peel with cornmeal or flour, or lightly coat a black pizza pan with olive oil.

Hand stretch or roll out dough into a 10-inch circle and place on peel or pan. Brush dough lightly with oil to cover completely.

Spread tomato sauce over dough, leaving a ½-inch border. Top with clams. Lightly salt; add a few grindings of black pepper, and oregano. Drizzle with 1 teaspoon oil and reserved clam juice.

Bake for 5 to 10 minutes, or until crust is golden. Serve with Spicy Oil (see page 30).

WHITE CLAM PIZZA

Prepared dough, enough for
  one 10-inch pizza
Olive oil
2 large garlic cloves,
  finely chopped
½ cup canned clams,
  drained (reserve
  2 teaspoons clam juice)

2 tablespoons freshly grated
  Parmesan cheese
½ teaspoon dried basil or
  oregano

LINE OVEN RACK with quarry tiles or pizza stone if using.
Preheat oven to 500°F for 1 hour.

Sprinkle peel with cornmeal or flour, or lightly coat a black
pizza pan with olive oil.

Hand stretch or roll out dough into a 10-inch circle and
place on peel or pan. Brush dough lightly with oil to cover
completely.

Spread garlic over dough, leaving a ½-inch border.
Top with clams and clam juice, Parmesan cheese, and basil.
Drizzle with 1 tablespoon olive oil.

Bake for 5 to 10 minutes, or until crust is golden.

If you are ever in New Haven, Connecticut, stop by Pepe's Pizzeria and try their delicious clam pie. It's nothing more than a light, chewy crust topped with fresh shucked clams, olive oil, and lots of garlic, that is baked in a huge coal-fired oven. It's nothing less than heaven. ♦ Here is my rendition. ♦ If you are lucky enough to have access to fresh littleneck clams, by all means substitute fresh shucked clams for the canned.

chicken

MEAT & POULTRY

PIZZAS

♦ ♦ ♦

Make this pizza with good-quality bacon, preferably purchased from a farmer's market or butcher, rather than the prepacked variety. ♦ Fresh bacon gives a subtle smoky taste without overpowering the other ingredients. ♦ Be sure to cook the bacon until it is beginning to crisp, or it will be under-cooked when the other toppings are ready.

BACON, RED ONION, AND TOMATO PIZZA

3 slices bacon, diced
Prepared dough, enough for one 10-inch pizza
Olive oil
1 cup grated mozzarella cheese
2 very thin slices red onion, separated into rings
1 large garlic clove, finely chopped
1 ripe medium tomato (about ¼ pound), seeded and diced
Salt
Freshly ground black pepper

LINE OVEN RACK with quarry tiles or pizza stone if using. Preheat oven to 500°F for 1 hour.

Sprinkle peel with cornmeal or flour, or lightly coat a black pizza pan with olive oil.

In a small skillet, cook bacon until just crisp; remove to a paper towel-lined plate to drain.

Hand stretch or roll out dough into a 10-inch circle and place on peel or pan. Brush dough lightly with oil to cover completely.

Spread cheese over dough, leaving a ½-inch border. Top with bacon, red onion, garlic, and tomato. Lightly salt and add a few grindings of black pepper.

Bake for 5 to 10 minutes, or until cheese is bubbly and crust is golden.

BRAISED GARLIC, PANCETTA, AND FRESH BASIL PIZZA

Olive oil
1 large head garlic (about 18 large cloves), peeled and left whole
Prepared dough, enough for one 10-inch pizza

5 ounces pancetta, thinly sliced and cut into thick julienne
Salt
Freshly ground black pepper
2 tablespoons shredded fresh basil leaves

LINE OVEN RACK with quarry tiles or pizza stone if using. Preheat oven to 500°F for 1 hour.

In a heavy small skillet, heat 2 tablespoons oil. Add garlic and cook on low heat for 15 to 30 minutes, or until garlic is soft but not browned. Set aside.

Sprinkle peel with cornmeal or flour, or lightly coat a black pizza pan with olive oil.

Hand stretch or roll out dough into a 10-inch circle and place on peel or pan.

Spread garlic mixture over dough, leaving a ½-inch border. Brush edges of dough lightly with oil. Top with pancetta Lightly salt and add a few grindings of pepper

Bake for 5 to 10 minutes, or until crust is golden.

Remove pizza from oven and sprinkle with basil.

onderful, elegant and simple — one of the stars in my pizza collection. ◆ You must have excellent pancetta, which is available in quality Italian meat markets that specialize in or (preferably) make their own prosciutto, sausages, and cured meats. ◆ Buy the pancetta thinly sliced; if you can't stop eating it out of the package before you get home, you've purchased the right stuff.

My husband, Drew, was raised in upstate New York and loves New York-style pizzas. Over the past twenty years, we've stopped in almost every pizzeria-bar we've come across while driving to New York City. Some of the pizzerias were pretty grotty looking, but we sure discovered some great pizzas. ◆ This is my rendition of a pizza we enjoyed several years ago. ◆ Meatballs on a pizza sounds like a crazy idea, but it's old-fashioned, hearty, and incredibly tasty. Serve with lots of ice-cold beer.

NEW YORK MEATBALL PIZZA

Meatballs:
¾ pound ground beef
¼ cup dry breadcrumbs
¼ cup freshly grated
  Parmesan cheese
1 large garlic clove, finely
  chopped
1 teaspoon dried oregano
1 large egg
Salt
Freshly ground black pepper
Olive oil for frying

Sauce:
2 tablespoons olive oil
4 large garlic cloves,
  chopped
28-ounce (796-mL) can
  tomatoes, undrained

5½-ounce (156-mL) can
  tomato paste
2 teaspoons dried oregano
2 teaspoons dried basil
¼ teaspoon hot red pepper
  flakes
6-inch cinnamon stick
Salt
½ teaspoon freshly ground
  black pepper
Prepared dough, enough for
  one 10-inch pizza
1 cup grated mozzarella
  cheese
1 cup grated provolone
  cheese
¼ teaspoon dried oregano

PREHEAT OVEN to 500°F for 1 hour. Lightly coat a black pizza pan with olive oil.

To make meatballs, in a large bowl, combine ground beef, breadcrumbs, Parmesan cheese, garlic, oregano, egg, salt, and pepper (your hands work best), but do not handle the mixture any more than you have to. Form mixture into meatballs about 1 inch in diameter.

In a large skillet, heat oil. Fry meatballs in two batches until browned. Drain and set aside.

To make sauce, in a noncorrosive medium saucepan, heat oil. Add garlic and cook for 2 minutes. Add tomatoes, tomato paste, oregano, basil, hot pepper flakes, cinnamon, salt, and pepper. Cook for 15 minutes on medium-low heat, stirring occasionally. Add meatballs and cook for 15 minutes more.

Hand stretch or roll out dough into a 10-inch circle and place on pan. Brush dough lightly with oil to cover completely.

Spread ½ cup mozzarella and ½ cup provolone over dough, leaving a ½-inch border. Scoop out 14 meatballs from sauce and place on cheese. Spread 1 cup tomato sauce over meatballs. (Save leftover sauce for tossing with pasta.) Cover with remaining cheese. Sprinkle with oregano. Lightly salt and add a few grindings of pepper.

Bake for 10 minutes, or until cheese is bubbly and lightly browned.

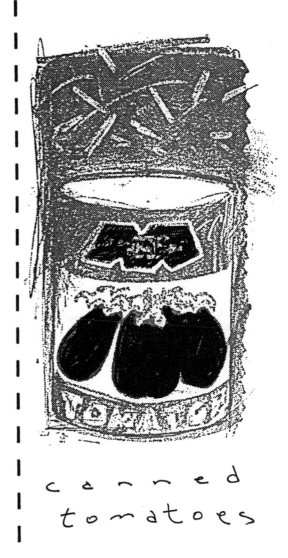

canned
tomatoes

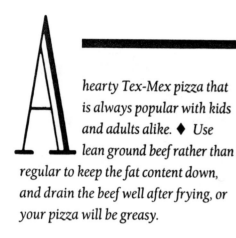

A hearty Tex-Mex pizza that is always popular with kids and adults alike. ◆ Use lean ground beef rather than regular to keep the fat content down, and drain the beef well after frying, or your pizza will be greasy.

CHILI PIZZA

Olive oil
4 large garlic cloves, chopped
1 small onion, finely chopped
⅓ pound lean ground beef
1 tablespoon good-quality chili powder
Salt
Freshly ground black pepper

Prepared dough, enough for one 10-inch pizza
1 cup grated Cheddar or Monterey Jack cheese
Sour cream
2 green onions, chopped
1 ripe medium tomato (about ¼ pound), seeded and diced
Chopped fresh coriander (optional)

PREHEAT OVEN to 500°F for 1 hour. Lightly coat a black pizza pan with olive oil.

In a heavy skillet, heat 1 tablespoon oil. Add garlic and onion and cook for 2 to 3 minutes, or until soft. Add beef, chili powder, salt, and a few grindings of pepper. Cook, breaking up beef with a fork, until no pink remains. Drain off excess fat and set aside.

Hand stretch or roll out dough into a 10-inch circle and place on pan. Brush dough lightly with oil to cover completely.

Spread ground beef mixture over dough, leaving a ½-inch border. Spread cheese over beef mixture.

Bake for 5 to 10 minutes, or until cheese is bubbly and crust is golden.

Remove pizza from oven. Top with a dollop of sour cream; garnish with green onions, tomato, and coriander if using. Pass extra sour cream.

ITALIAN SAUSAGE AND HOT PEPPER PIZZA

⅓ pound Italian sausage, casing removed
Prepared dough, enough for one 10-inch pizza
Olive oil
½ cup No-Cook Tomato Sauce (see page 27)
1 cup grated mozzarella cheese

1 to 2 tablespoons hot pickled pepper rings, drained
Salt
Freshly ground black pepper

LINE OVEN RACK with quarry tiles or pizza stone if using. Preheat oven to 500°F for 1 hour.

Sprinkle peel with cornmeal or flour, or lightly coat a black pizza pan with olive oil.

In a heavy medium skillet, cook sausage, breaking it up with a fork, until no pink remains. Remove with a slotted spoon to a paper towel-lined plate to drain.

Hand stretch or roll out dough into a 10-inch circle and place on peel or pan. Brush dough lightly with oil to cover completely.

Spread tomato sauce over dough, leaving a ½-inch border. Spread cheese over sauce. Top with sausage and pepper rings. Lightly salt and add a few grindings of black pepper.

Bake for 5 to 10 minutes, or until cheese is bubbly and crust is golden.

I talian sausage and hot pickled peppers are a popular topping in many New York pizzerias, but this pizza is also delicious without the hot peppers. ◆ Many people like to add chopped green pepper, mushrooms, and double cheese. If you use only the best Italian sausage — either hot or mild — you won't need the extra embellishments.

first tasted chicken pizza at The Spot in New Haven, Connecticut. ◆ I felt it had potential but needed a little extra something, so when I got home I tried grilling the chicken before adding it to my pizza. The charcoal flavor was just what it needed!

GRILLED CHICKEN AND MUSHROOM PIZZA

Prepared dough, enough for one 10-inch pizza
Olive oil
1 cup grated mozzarella cheese
1 cup shredded grilled chicken breast
2 ounces fresh mushrooms, thinly sliced (about 1 cup)

1 very thin slice red onion, separated into rings
½ teaspoon dried basil or oregano
Salt
Freshly ground black pepper
2 tablespoons freshly grated Romano cheese

PREHEAT OVEN to 500°F for 1 hour.

Lightly coat a black pizza pan with olive oil.

Hand stretch or roll out dough into a 10-inch circle and place on pan. Brush dough lightly with oil to cover completely.

Spread mozzarella cheese over dough, leaving a ½-inch border. Place chicken, mushrooms, and onions over cheese. Sprinkle with basil, salt, and a few grindings of black pepper.

Bake for 5 to 10 minutes, or until crust is golden and cheese is bubbling.

Remove pizza from oven and sprinkle with Romano cheese.

CHINESE BARBECUED PORK PIZZA

Prepared Thin and Crispy
  Dough, enough for one
  10-inch pizza
¾ teaspoon sesame oil
2 tablespoons hoisin sauce
5 ounces char siu (barbecued
  pork), cut into thin strips

6 fresh shiitake mushrooms,
  stems removed, cut into
  thin strips
8 fresh water chestnuts,
  peeled and sliced into
  3 rounds
¼ teaspoon vegetable oil
1 large green onion (green
  part only), slivered

LINE OVEN RACK with quarry tiles or pizza stone if using. Preheat oven to 500°F for 1 hour.

Sprinkle peel with cornmeal or flour, or lightly coat a black pizza pan with olive oil.

Hand stretch or roll out dough into a 10-inch circle and place on peel or pan. Brush dough lightly with ¼ teaspoon sesame oil to cover completely.

Spread hoisin sauce over dough, leaving a ½-inch border. Top with pork, mushrooms, and water chestnuts. Drizzle with ¼ teaspoon sesame oil and ¼ teaspoon vegetable oil.

Bake for 5 minutes, or until crust is golden. Watch carefully because topping will dry out if cooked too long.

Remove pizza from oven. Drizzle with ¼ teaspoon sesame oil and sprinkle with green onions.

N*ovel and so delicious, with the flavor and textural contrasts of sweet hoisin sauce and barbecued pork, mushrooms, water chestnuts, and green onions — very similar to mu shu pork.* ◆ *Serve in wedges as an appetizer or first course.* ◆ *The ingredients are available in Chinese barbecue shops and grocery stores.*

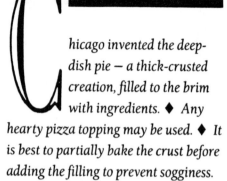

Chicago invented the deep-dish pie — a thick-crusted creation, filled to the brim with ingredients. ◆ Any hearty pizza topping may be used. ◆ It is best to partially bake the crust before adding the filling to prevent sogginess. ◆ This combination is also wonderful on a thin crust — just halve the filling ingredients.

DEEP-DISH LAMB AND EGGPLANT PIZZA

Olive oil
2 Japanese eggplants (½ pound), unpeeled and sliced
½ pound ground lamb
1 medium onion, thinly sliced
2 large garlic cloves, chopped
1 pound prepared dough
28-ounce (796-mL) can tomatoes, drained and crushed
1 teaspoon dried oregano
1 teaspoon dried thyme
½ pound soft goat cheese, crumbled
Salt
Freshly ground black pepper

PREHEAT OVEN to 450°F for 1 hour.

In a large heavy skillet, heat about 1 tablespoon olive oil. Add eggplant and cook for 5 minutes, or until soft. Remove to a plate.

In same skillet, add a little more oil if necessary and heat. Add lamb, onion, and garlic, and cook until no pink remains. Drain well and remove to a plate.

Lightly coat a black deep-dish pizza pan (15 inches) with oil. Roll out dough and press into deep-dish pan. Prick bottom with tines of a fork.

Bake for 5 minutes.

Remove pizza and brush dough lightly with olive oil to cover completely.

Spread the lamb mixture over bottom of crust. Top with eggplant, then crushed tomatoes. Sprinkle with oregano and thyme. Top with goat cheese. Drizzle with 2 teaspoons oil, and lightly salt and pepper.

Bake for 25 minutes, or until cheese is bubbly and crust is golden.

PEPPERONI PIZZA

Prepared dough, enough for
  one 10-inch pizza
Olive oil
½ cup No-Cook Tomato
  Sauce (see page 27)
1½ cups grated mozzarella
  cheese

10 to 15 very thin slices
  pepperoni or Genoa
  sausage, depending on
  size
½ teaspoon dried oregano
Salt
Freshly ground black pepper

LINE OVEN RACK with quarry tiles or pizza stone if using. Preheat oven to 500°F for 1 hour.

Sprinkle peel with cornmeal or flour, or lightly coat a black pizza pan with olive oil.

Hand stretch or roll out dough into a 10-inch circle and place on peel or pan. Brush dough lightly with oil to cover completely.

Spread tomato sauce over dough, leaving a ½-inch border. Spread ½ cup cheese over sauce. Top with pepperoni or Genoa sausage, then with remaining cheese. Sprinkle with oregano. Lightly salt and add a few grindings of pepper.

Bake for 5 to 10 minutes, or until cheese is bubbling and crust is golden

A merica's all-time favorite topping. ♦ The best pizzerias have access to quality Italian cured meat suppliers, but it is very difficult for the home cook to find excellent pepperoni that doesn't taste salty. Try different brands until you find a pepperoni that you like, or purchase Genoa sausage, which is much easier to find. ♦ The cheese is placed both under and over the sausage, so that the slices won't curl or dry out.

INDEX

◆ ◆ ◆

INDEX